S0-AHW-562

Quench!

Quench!

refreshing devotionals by gay, trans, and affirming Christians

edited by Rev. Keith J. Phillips

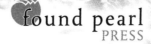

found pearl
PRESS

© 2009 by Found Pearl Press. All rights reserved.

Published 2009. Printed in the United States of America.

Unless otherwise noted, all Scripture quotations are taken from the *New Revised Standard Version Bible.*

Quotations from the *New Revised Standard Version Bible,* copyright © 1989 by the Division of Christian Education of the National Council of Churches of Christ in the U.S.A., are used by permission. All rights reserved.

A RETURN TO LOVE by MARIANNE WILLIAMSON. Copyright © 1992 by Marianne Williamson. Reprinted by permission of HarperCollins Publishers.

THE HOUSE AT POOH CORNER by A. A. Milne, copyright 1928 by E.P. Dutton, renewed © 1956 by A.A. Milne. Used by permission of Dutton Children's Books, A Division of Penguin Young Readers Group, A Member of Penguin Group (USA) Inc., 345 Hudson Street, New York, NY 10014. All rights reserved.

Still, Words and Music by Reuben Morgan. © 2002 Reuben Morgan and Hillsong Publishing (admin. in the U.S. and Canada by Integrity's Hosanna! Music)/ASCAP, c/o Integrity Meida, Inc., 1000 Cody Road, Mobile, AL 36695 All rights reserved. International Copyright Secured. Used by Permission.

Design by David Squire.

Dedication and Acknowledgments

This book is dedicated to Brad Burton, who by his friendship at the opportune time brought refreshment which has changed everything for me. Thank you, Brad.

I also wish to thank a number of friends, all of whom are members of the Found Pearl Press Ministry Team at Jesus Metropolitan Community Church, Indianapolis, and each of whom made my work as editor of this book a little bit easier:

Rev. Jeff Miner, Pastor of Jesus MCC, whose vision and sense of mission transforms so much; David Squire, Communications Director of Jesus MCC, who from the beginning has coordinated and edited the online edition of *Be Still and Know,* from which these devotions were taken, and who designed and facilitated the production of *Quench!*; Grant Mabie, who mentored me in editorship and set a high standard; Lynn Adams, who produced the index; Mark Shoup, Administrative Assistant of Jesus MCC, who acquired necessary permissions; Albert Hidalgo, who provided marketing insight in the nick of time; Richard Felton, who kept us accountable; and Lynne Kaminski, the fearless leader of our Ministry Team. Thank you, all. And thanks be to God!

—Keith

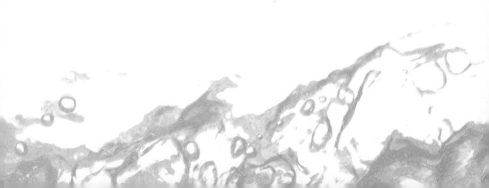

Introduction

This is not your typical book of daily devotions for Christians. It may be unlike any such book you have ever read.

Yes, the concept is familiar. Each day you can use this book for some quality time in developing your relationship with God — meditate on a passage of scripture, read our reflections, and talk with God about how to use both your thoughts and our thoughts in your life.

But this book is different because of its unique group of writers. We are more like *you* than most writers of these sorts of books:

☛ We are Christians who are lesbian, gay, transgender, or straight and affirming. In that sense, we are all queer, although some of us don't much care for that word.

☛ The majority of us are lay people, although a few have been to Bible college or seminary.

☛ We come with very diverse theological viewpoints, from extremely progressive to quite evangelical.

But all of us love God deeply, knowing that God loved us first; and we want to walk closer to God each day. We all write for an online

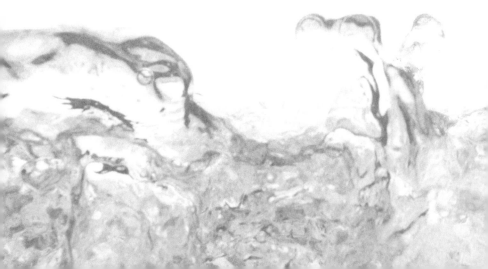

devotional, *Be Still and Know,* which Jesus Metropolitan Community Church, in Indianapolis, Indiana, has produced since May 2006.

Sometimes you'll find that the day's focus is specifically LGBTQ (lesbian/gay/bisexual/transgender/queer). Most of the time, though, we are simply writing as Christians for those who are seeking something spiritually refreshing for our souls in these times.

We come to God just as you do. We are unapologetic about being followers of Jesus. We believe that God knows who we are to the core of our being, loves us unconditionally, and accepts us just as we are, desiring that we become more like Jesus.

We believe that we can best follow Jesus when we welcome diversity and independent thought, and when we're open to truth, recognizing that none of us has the whole truth this side of eternity.

Jesus said to the Samaritan woman at the well,

> But those who drink of the water that I will give them will never be thirsty. The water that I will give will become in them a spring of water gushing up to eternal life. (John 4:14)

We hope that our thoughts will help quench your spiritual thirst day-by-day, and that the living water of God will pour into and through your life, to the glory of God.

Contents

How to use this book

Each of the 100 entries in this book has three parts:

☞ Today's Scripture. After you read the day's passage, we recommend you take some time to meditate on it and ask yourself, *What might God be saying to me from this? Does any word, phrase, or idea stand out?* It may help to summarize your thoughts in a sentence or two before reading on.

☞ Our Thoughts. The authors will share what they have taken from the scripture.

☞ Thought for the Day. This is something you can take with you, to remember and ponder throughout the day.

We also suggest that you include **a time of prayer** with your reading. *Appendix 1* offers some thoughts and suggestions for effective prayer.

1. *Fear This!*
by Tyler Connoley

Today's scripture: Psalm 34:1–11

There was a time in my life when I would have looked upon starting a daily devotional with a sense of dread. I felt obligated to do it, but I didn't think I'd be able to keep it up. I was sure I'd fail and let God down, and that would result in my being sent off to hell as soon as I died.

Then I'd read a passage like Psalm 34 and get stuck on verse 11: "Come, oh children, listen to me; I will teach you the fear of the Lord."

Fear. That's what Christianity used to be about for me — fear of hell, of God, of the Church, and, most of all, fear of not living up to all the rules and regulations that came with True Christianity as I understood it. I had this idea that God was like an evil dog trainer who enjoyed making his dogs jump through flaming hoops, just so he could show how much power he had over them.

The Hebrew word in verse 11, usually translated "fear," has more of a sense of respecting God — of standing in awe of God. Today, I picture God as a loving mother who makes rules, like "brush your

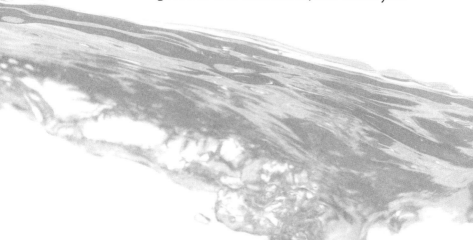

teeth every night," because she knows it will help her children grow stronger and healthier. God wants us to succeed in life, and to be the best we can be. And when God asks us to do something, it's because it will help us. When we forget to follow God's rules, like a child who forgets to brush her teeth before bed, God doesn't throw us out of the house. God reminds us, again, why the rule is good.

Now I spend time with God because I'm learning the pleasure of listening to the One who knows me like a perfect mother and wants what's best for me. I fear/respect God as the greatest source of wisdom and power in my life.

> **Thought for the day:** As you go through the day, think about God wanting what's best for you in every situation. Then try to follow God's path, respecting the One who knows you best and wants what's best for you.

2. *How Far Is East?*
by David Squire

Today's scripture: Psalm 103

Remember Jacob Marley, from Dickens's *A Christmas Carol?* Even if you've never read the story, you've probably seen ten thousand and two versions of it on television in the month before Christmas. Jacob was the first ghost to visit Mr. Scrooge and, in life, had been Scrooge's business partner.

Ol' Jacob carried around all the baggage he had accumulated in this life. In fact, it was chained to him — he couldn't get away from it.

What's chained to you? What festers in the corners of your heart? Maybe it's a relationship that ended badly, or something you've said that you can't take back. Maybe it was something that couldn't be avoided — like causing a loved one pain when you came out to them. If you've done your best to make it right, do you find yourself still "chained" to the guilt, dragging it around like Jacob and his burdens?

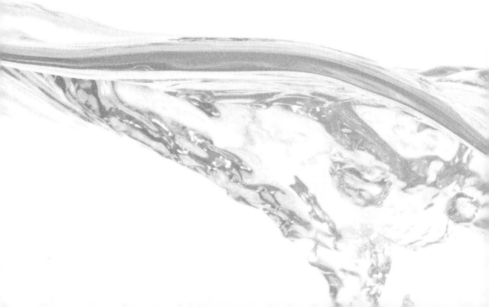

If you're anything like me, I don't like to think about it — "out of sight, out of mind" is a motto I can live by. But every so often I'm reminded, and the chains begin to rattle.

But verses 11–12 from this psalm give me hope:

God does not deal with us according to our sins, nor repay us according to our iniquities. For as the heavens are high above the earth, so great is God's steadfast love toward those who fear God; as far as the east is from the west, so far God removes our transgressions from us.

It's interesting that the writer didn't say "as far as the north is from the south." You can only go a finite distance north — then you start heading back south again. East and west, however, are infinitely far apart. (If this doesn't make intuitive sense, check out the lines on a globe. You can go east or west forever.)

So when I confess/repent/give it to God, it's really gone. And if God moves my baggage infinitely far away, what business do I have yanking the chains to bring it back? Just let it be.

"As far as the east is from the west..."

Thought for the day: What guilt is still chained to you? *Let it go.*

3. *There Goes the Neighborhood!*
by Jeff Miner

Today's scripture: Luke 7:1–10

One of Jesus' favorite sayings, oft repeated in the Gospels, is this: "The last will be first, and the first will be last" (Matthew 29:16). Today's Gospel story is a classic example of that principle at work.

Remember, Jesus was born into the Jewish nation at a time of great upheaval. The Roman Empire had conquered Israel. To maintain their power, the Romans stationed large numbers of soldiers there. Any sign of uprising was dealt with fiercely. Any Jew suspected of challenging Roman authority was ruthlessly executed on a cross. These public executions were meant to send a blunt message: Don't mess with Rome!

If you had been a Jew in Jesus' day, how would you have felt about those who were part of the Roman war machine?

In this story, a Roman centurion, who led a unit of at least 100 soldiers, found himself so desperate for a miracle that he dared to ask a leader among the people he was oppressing (Jesus) for help. Why was this centurion so desperate? He had a sick slave.

Wait a minute! That doesn't sound very plausible. This was a time in history when slaves were viewed as chattel, mere property. Slaves were used until they were used up, then tossed aside. It was easier to buy a new slave than to invest time and money in trying to fix a

broken one. So why was this grizzled warrior so concerned about a mere slave?

Because this wasn't a "mere" slave. When translated literally from its original Greek into English — without rearranging the syntax to make for smooth English — Luke 7:2 reads as follows: "Now of a certain centurion certain a slave ill having was about to die, who was to him dear" (*The NIV Interlinear Greek-English New Testament* [*Zondervan, 1976*]). There are two key words here. The sick man was a "slave" (Greek = *doulos*) who was "dear" (Greek = *entimos*) to the centurion.

And why was this slave so dear to the centurion? The answer is found in verse 7, the only portion of our passage where the actual words of the centurion are reported. In the original Greek, the centurion refers to the sick slave who was dear to him as his *pais* (*The NIV Interlinear Greek-English New Testament*). "Only speak the word," the centurion says to Jesus, "and let my servant [*pais*] be healed."

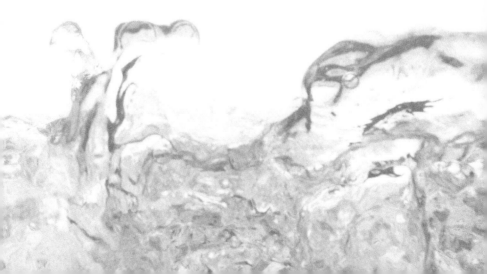

There are hundreds of instances in ancient Greek literature in which *"pais"* is used as the term of choice to refer to one's same-sex partner (K. J. Dover. *Greek Homosexuality* [Harvard University Press, Cambridge, 1978], p. 16; Bernard Sergent. *Homosexuality in Greek Myth* [Beacon Press, Boston, 1986], p. 10). In the ancient world, it was not uncommon for officers in the Roman army (and other powerful men) to acquire male slaves to serve as their lovers. This sounds awfully primitive, and it was. But remember, under the laws of the time, men who married women also "acquired" them as "property." Unfortunately, that's how the ancient world worked — for both straight and gay folks.

So now we have the complete picture. If we were to sum up the situation presented in Luke 7 through the eyes of a typical Jew at the time, here's what we would say: "One of our chief oppressors, an officer in the Roman war machine — a Gentile dog, a pagan pervert — is asking our Jesus to salvage his perverted relationship by healing his love slave. How presumptuous! How disgusting! Has he no shame!"

And how does Jesus react? Does he squint his eyes and sneer in judgment? Does he fly into a tirade about Roman sexual perversion?

Well, actually, no. Verse 9 records Jesus' reaction: "When Jesus heard this he was amazed at [the centurion]. Jesus turned to the crowd that followed him and said, 'I tell you, not even among the Jews have I found such faith.'" Jesus granted the miracle of healing, preserving the relationship between the centurion and his *pais*.

So there we have it. A Roman centurion was so in love with one of his slaves that he broke through all kinds of social boundaries to ask Jesus, a Jew, for help — convinced that the power of God rested so completely in Jesus that he could heal his servant by merely speaking a word. Unconcerned about the obvious homosexual nature of this relationship, Jesus announces that this soldier has greater faith than any Jew he has ever met.

Think about that! Jesus saw more faith in a gay Roman soldier than in all the holy men and woman of Israel. And you know what the Bible says about faith: "By grace you are saved, through faith" (Ephesians 2:8). Heaven sure is going to be an interesting place!

Thought for the day: Don't get stuck on superficial issues (like sexual orientation); focus on what really matters to Jesus — how much faith you have. For the first shall be last and the last shall be first.

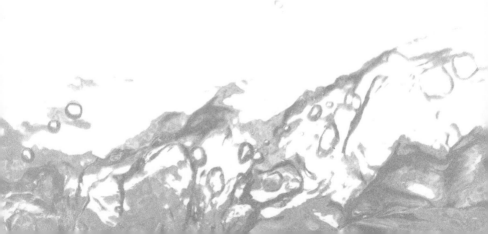

4. *Power Source*
by Melody Merida

Today's scripture: 2 Timothy 1:7–10

When I was in high school, I attended a small, ultra-conservative Christian church and school. We students were told that we needed to look and act different from the kids in town who attended the public school. Some of us had to struggle to act differently, but boy did we succeed at looking different! I remember begging my mother to let me wear a pair of jeans instead of a long skirt. I wanted to be normal like everyone else!

And we didn't go unnoticed. Most folks in our town knew where we went to church and school because of our different appearance. For most of my high school years, I was terribly embarrassed of looking different. I was ashamed of my faith traditions that called upon me to be different. I felt timid and shy when I went outside of my social circles. A trip to the grocery store with my mother would make me a nervous wreck. Because of this, I rarely ventured outside of my

own group of peers. I made it a purpose not to go anywhere without a large group of friends who looked like me. There was strength in numbers. I didn't feel quite so ashamed if my friends were with me.

When I look back on this time in my life, I realize that most of my anxiety probably had nothing to do with what other people thought. Most people in the community couldn't have cared less about how I dressed and looked. It was my perception that caused me to be so embarrassed.

I'm not saying that we should adopt the specific principles that guided my family when I was young, but I am saying we shouldn't be embarrassed about our faith and what our faith calls us to do in service to our Lord.

Today's scripture tells us that God gave us the spirit of power, not of timidity. Because of our power found in Christ, we shouldn't be ashamed to testify about our Lord. In fact, we should be thrilled to show others that the Creator God is our power source.

Thought for the day: Am I living a timid life or a life filled with power? The spirit of fear is not from God — so tap into God's ultimate power source.

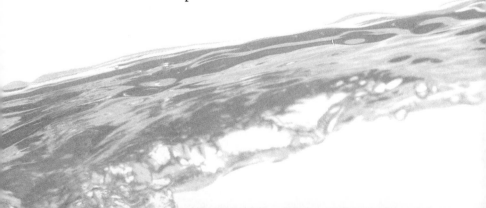

5. *In Its Own Time*
by Theresa Benson

Today's scripture: Ecclesiastes 3:1–11

When I was single in Oregon and trying to figure out how to date "as a grown up" (versus a college kid, with guys to meet in pretty much every class or at every Greek event), I came across a cleverly titled book called, *If the Buddha Dated.*

One of the best pieces of advice that book gave me was: "Don't be hung up on where it might go!" In other words, rather than going on that first date and then starting to imagine a whole life together — would this guy be a good father to my children, would my friends like him, etc. — just enjoy the date for the date, and let the process unfold.

My best friend in California, who is transgender, has a weekly podcast that I adore, and she always signs off the same way:

Show up,
Tell the truth,
Pay attention,
And don't be attached to the outcome.

Here is one of my favorite scriptures, saying the same thing — "Everything is appropriate in its own time." I work daily on learning how not to be attached to making something happen a certain way just because I think it should happen that way. God has a plan, there's a time for everything, and I need to enjoy this life that God's given me — and quit getting emotionally wrapped up in wanting something to turn out a certain way, and then being sorely disappointed when it doesn't.

There will be a time to find, lose, keep, and throw away. Don't be hung up on forcing this time to be what you think it should be. Let God, who knows a lot more than any of us, make it the time it's supposed to be; and let us, as my friend Robin says, show up and pay attention so we can enjoy this moment before we move on to the next.

Thought for the day: God, am I allowing you to move in this moment? Or am I just getting in the way?

6. *Courage!*
by David Zier

Today's scripture: Exodus 17:8–12

When I was diagnosed with a brain tumor in May 1993, I was in shock. We walked to the car after the appointment, and Jeff and I just sat there in the car and cried in each other's arms. I remember crying out, "Why did God let this happen to me?"

Over the next week, Jeff carefully put together a daily devotional notebook filled with pictures of himself and our pets, cards, scripture readings, and prayers. It was the daily encouragement I needed to get back on spiritual track for the battle I faced in the coming weeks and months.

In the Exodus passage, the Israelites are in the middle of their battle against the Amalekites. Moses went up to the top of the hill and placed himself so as to be seen by the army. There he held up "the staff of God in his hand" — the staff that had worked so

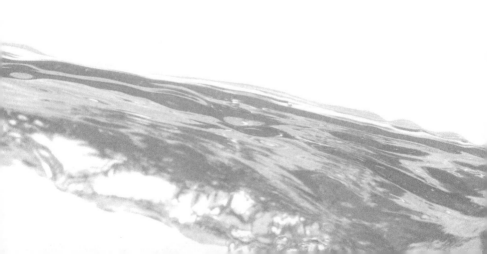

many miracles before. The staff was held up as the banner of God to encourage the soldiers, who might look up and think, "God is with us, God is on our side, and Moses, our leader, is strengthening us with prayers to God." Moses was an intercessor, pleading with God for success and victory. The spiritual focus and energy of the task caused Moses' hands to grow weary. He could no longer keep the staff raised, so Aaron and Hur held his hands up, and together they prayed to God and lifted the staff for Israel's victory.

During my brain tumor ordeal, my "staff" was the devotional book that Jeff put together for me. Every day, we would pray from that book. My faith was strengthened, and I knew that God was with me. It was there with me in the hospital where I would go through it many times a day, then during my recovery at home, and through to my victory. We should all strive to be an encouragement of faith to others, and to reflect upon the great things God has done for us.

Thought for the day: Whom can I encourage today?

7. *Remember Who You Are*
by Tommy Chittenden

Today's scripture: Mark 10:13–16

Perhaps you have heard the story of when Michelangelo was asked how he created a piece of sculpture. He answered that the statue already existed within the marble. God had created the Pieta, David, and Moses. Michelangelo's job, as he saw it, was to get rid of the excess marble that surrounded God's creation.

And so it is with us. The perfect "you" isn't something you need to create, because God has already created it. The perfect you is the unconditional love within you. Your job is to allow the Holy Spirit to remove the fearful thinking, limiting beliefs, wrong conclusions about the past, and any other negatives that surround your perfect self, just like the excess marble surrounding Michelangelo's perfect statue.

I love this thought, from Marianne Williamson's book, *A Return to Love:*

> To remember that we are part of God, that we are loved and lovable, is not arrogant. It's humble. To think we are anything else is arrogant, because it implies we're something other than a creation of God. Nothing we have ever done or will ever do can mar our perfection in the eyes of God. We are deserving in God's eyes because of what we are, not because of what we do.

What we do or don't do is not what determines our essential value — our personal growth perhaps, but not our value! That's why God approves and accepts us, exactly as we are. What's not to like? *We were not created in sin; we were created in love!*

And so, in reality, our personal spiritual journey, ironic as it sounds, isn't so much a journey *toward* as it is a *return* to love — that pure, simple, guiltless, perfect love that we came into the world possessing. It's time to "remember who we are." It's time to invoke the magnificent power of the Holy Spirit and exercise our free will by telling God that we are willing to look at our lives, our circumstances, our feelings, our relationships differently. This "different look," with consistent focus and intention, will allow the Spirit to bring healing light into our heart and mind. This light will dissolve away all that is not truth, all that is not love, returning us to the true essence of Christ — one with him! Then we will experience God's peace, the peace that cannot be put into words.

If the things you have been doing and the way you have been thinking have not yielded the changes you desire in your life and your world, then perhaps it is time to think and do things differently!

Thought for the day: Remind me, God, that you created me in love, in your image. I have everything I need to overcome the fears that have accumulated in my life. I have access to the wellspring of perfect love.

8. *Whithersoever Thou Goest*
by Keith Phillips

Today's scripture: Joshua 1:1–9

It was more than 30 years ago, but I remember it as though it were yesterday. I'd hitched a ride with a friend who was going to Seattle. Two months earlier we'd both graduated from college in Massachusetts. He dropped me off, with all my worldly possessions, in Richmond, Indiana, where I'd been accepted to seminary, having never even seen the campus. I got there two weeks early. I knew no one, but it didn't matter; no one else was around.

In those days a few single students were housed on the second floor of the classroom building. Through the attic was a cupola which I quickly discovered to be a wonderful place to talk with God; and, quite frankly, to express my loneliness, my fears about being in a strange land (you may not believe it, but Indiana can be pretty strange for those of us from New England), and my questions about seminary and my call to ministry. I felt like I was in a desert. I'd been uprooted. I was young, I was gay, I was a Deadhead, and now I was in a Midwestern seminary; and I had no idea what, in the early '70s, all that might mean for me. I felt scared, I felt alone, I felt abandoned.

One afternoon I had my Bible with me in that cupola, and by chance, or by the grace of God, I opened it to the first chapter of

Joshua. I read the ninth verse in the King James Version:

> Have not I commanded thee? Be strong and of a good courage; be not afraid, neither be thou dismayed: for the Lord thy God is with thee whithersoever thou goest.

It was as though God were speaking those words directly to me. God *was* speaking those words directly to me! And, as if I were passing through a gate into another world, a sense of serenity came over me, and I knew that everything would be all right.

Since that time, I have paraphrased that verse as a continual reminder: "Don't be afraid, Keith; stand by the Lord, and the Lord will walk with you." The journey certainly has had some wandering; and it's been full of detours and not a few battles, much like Joshua's journey into the Promised Land. But the Lord's promise has been true, and I have no regrets. I have done my best to stand by the Lord, and the Lord has been with me all along the way.

Thought for the day: Be assured that, whether you sense the Lord's presence or not, the Lord is with you, today and always.

9. *Your Difference Makes the Difference*
by Tyler Connoley

Today's scripture: Esther 4:1–17

This is the turning point in the story of Esther. Before this chapter, the wicked Haman has tried to annihilate all Jews by writing a law making it legal to kill Jews and take their property on the 13th day of Adar. After this chapter, Esther will save the Jews from the impending holocaust by going to the king to change the law on behalf of her people. But, before that can happen, Cousin Mordecai must make Esther aware of the danger. He has to get a message into the king's harem, where he's not allowed to go because he's a man, and from which Esther can't leave. How can he do such a thing? Who can take the message?

Enter Hathach, a eunuch employed in the harem.

In the ancient near east, eunuchs were given special boundary-crossing abilities: they were allowed to pass between the worlds of men and women; they served in temples, guarding the sacred spaces from the profane; they were even employed to guard the tombs of famous people, marking the boundary between the living and the dead. A big reason for this boundary-crossing power was a eunuch's status as "neither a man nor a woman." In a real sense, eunuchs were the original transgender community.

And, in the book of Esther, a eunuch is the pivotal character who makes the salvation of the Jews possible. Without Hathach, the message would never have gotten to Esther, and she couldn't have gone to the king. Hathach is the hero of Esther 4:1–17 for the simple reason that Hathach is able to cross into the women's world (the harem) and back again. That's why this is one of my favorite scripture passages.

Hathach is a reminder that all of us have a role to play, and that often the thing that makes us most different is what makes us most necessary. It's also a strong affirmation for those of us who are gender-variant. Think about it this way, if it hadn't been for the gender-variant Hathach, the Jews would have all been killed — there would be no Jewish people, and there could have been no Jesus. That's quite an affirmation of Hathach's importance.

> **Thought for the day:** Take a few minutes to think about what makes you different, because that's a key to knowing how God will use you most powerfully. God made you just as you are for a purpose that only you can fulfill.

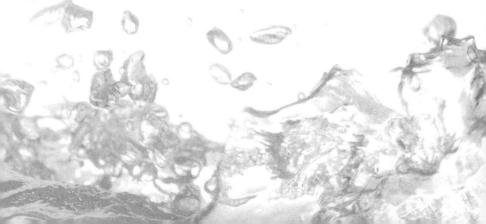

10. *Thanks, Aunt Clara!*
by Ben Lamb

Today's scripture: Matthew 6:19–21

One of the best presents I ever received taught me more about myself and about life than many of my college courses. One Christmas, Great-Aunt Clara presented me with a pair of thick, tan, cotton socks.

Some family members and I went to visit the sweet lady and her collie in their modest home during the late 1960s. I could hardly wait to open the loot that she would shower upon us.

Then it happened. In front of everyone, I unwrapped a pair of dime-store socks. They couldn't have cost more than 79 cents, and they were thick, too: the extra material would squeeze my feet inside my shoes. And they were tan: there'd be no hiding those monstrosities! A gift like this was at best a necessity — like underwear or toothpaste — and certainly not something "good." Still, I was able to force out a "thank you" to her.

It was months before I condescended to wear those wretched things, and only because I had no other choice that day. I just knew the whole world would hang motionless in suspended time, gasping in horror as I lumbered around school, trying to hide those socks.

Later, I discovered that after the initial washing, they were the softest socks I'd ever worn. I don't know what treatment those cotton threads received, but they were almost like silk! I convinced myself that I could wear them a little more often — but only with my longest pants, of course — and nobody would be the wiser about them.

Shortly thereafter, I got a pair of shoes that rubbed one of my heels. No matter what Dad and I tried, we couldn't get the mysterious problem solved as to why the one spot sometimes rubbed. But the thickness of the socks eliminated the rubbing. I was genuinely sad when they became too threadbare to keep.

After Great-Aunt Clara died in her 80s, I learned that she was very close to having to rely on government assistance to meet her living expenses. She was a proud woman (in the good and noble sense) who had helped others all her life. For her to have to depend on assistance would have been a heartbreaking embarrassment to her. I then better appreciated the sacrifices she must have made in order to give presents of any cost to so many of her relatives at Christmas. But she never complained when giving them to us.

I'm now ashamed of how I acted in my heart when unwrapping those socks — and, in retrospect, I wouldn't trade them for the world. Those socks taught me:

- Monetary worth doesn't measure true value.

- Don't be quick to judge a situation.

- We don't always know why people do what they do.

- Greed is ugly.

- It's never too late to admit my mistakes.

- God can use insignificant things as valuable learning tools.

Thank you, Aunt Clara, for those beautiful socks!

Thought for the day: Sock it to me, Lord, when I need a reminder of what's really important in this life!

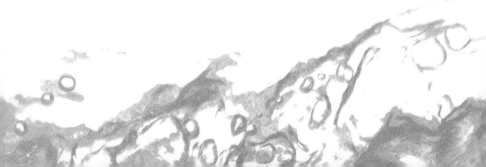

11. *My Life Sucks*
by Tommy Chittenden

Today's scripture: Psalm 4:6–8

"There are many who say, 'O that we might see some good!'" These phrases no doubt sound familiar to all of us:

Can it get any worse?
I can't believe this is happening to me!
This must be what the bottom of the barrel looks like.

Your turn — fill in the blank with one of your favorite "woe is me" sayings. Have you ever had the experience of talking with someone about "how terrible things are with you," saying something like, "you'll never believe what happened now"? You fully expect them to nod gently, affirming your words and feelings. You don't even mind when they interrupt to share their own "I'm a victim, too!" story.

Wait a minute! Did I hear you correctly? Did you say "victim"? Earlier this year, I wanted to slap "a voice of compassion and truth" who said to me, "My friend, I know your story. I know all about your life. What I only want to know is how would you like today and all of your tomorrows to look?"

Awkward silence. But my life hasn't been the same since that day. It was time to make a choice. Do I volunteer to remain a "victim" to mishaps, tragedies, and calamities? Do I allow a self-fulfilling prophecy to manifest and sabotage my tomorrows by repelling love, deferring happiness, attracting illness or injuries, and even pronouncing a death sentence on my financial or business success? I had been selling my "victim" story so well to everyone that I had become an expert at following the script.

My programming created my core beliefs, which directed the development of my vision for my life. Here's the kicker — that vision has been creating the results that conformed to it! "As a man thinks, so is he" became a phrase of meaning for me.

Every day seems to bring incredible truth regarding those aspects of life that typically generated negative feelings, thoughts, and conversations. Paul in Philippians 4:4–9 must have understood when he instructed the Christians about the power of thought as the key to gaining inner peace and joy. That joy will eventually crowd out the weeds and bring light to the shadows in the garden of our minds.

Do this little exercise and see what comes of it: Think of all of those "woe is me" memories that have imprisoned you and dictated your future life. Who is the one person who was always present at each broken relationship, at each failed business or miserable job, and at every illness or issue that prompts the "my life sucks" announcement? Could it possibly be that we have chosen to be the architect of our own "victimhood"?

You and I are children of the Creator of the universe. Don't you think this Absolute Power can equip you and me with the energy to rise above and to think on those spiritual truths and values which will guard our hearts and minds, enable us to overcome, and recognize our value? Our today and all of our tomorrows depend on our spiritual mentality. And our ability to be disciples of our Lord is absolutely dependent on our own spiritual health. As the Psalmist noted, "I will both lie down and sleep in peace."

Thought for the day: Lord Jesus, bring peace and harmony to my thoughts, let me confront any beliefs I have that are lies, that keep me in fear, depressed, and in low self-esteem. Through your Spirit, awaken me to the truth that I can do anything — including choosing to think, believe, and act like an overcomer!

12. *When Bad Christians Happen to Good People* by Julie Walsh

Today's scripture: Matthew 28:16–20

Over the years I've talked to several people who have been offended by Christians who have shown a bad example of Christian living. This may seem especially true in the LGBTQ community, where folks have been Bible-beaten and abused. One bad influence can affect a person's mentality for a lifetime.

So what do we do? Well, we definitely don't have to defend the behavior of those offensive Christians. Inconsistent or hypocritical Christians should never be a threat to sharing Christ with someone. Instead, we can turn the conversation into an opportunity to express the very reason why we all need him.

Personally, I am not a Christian because I think other Christians exemplify ideal behavior or represent the perfect model of humanity. I am a Christian because of what Jesus Christ has done for me. So why not share what we do know about Christianity and talk about Jesus instead? Who was he, and who is he today? What can Christ do for anyone who believes?

We don't have to prove that "our guys" are better than "their guys." We can encourage our friends to keep the focus on Jesus and

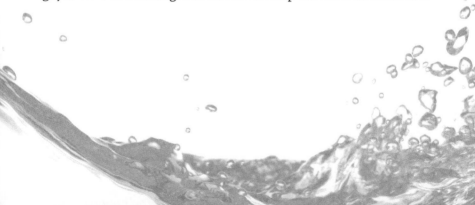

the need for him in our lives. We can acknowledge their concerns by saying something like, "Yeah, I know there are some pretty lousy Christian examples out there. But it's not about Christians; it's about Christ."

Let's get a quick reality check: We'd all be in trouble if it was just about Christians — even the original twelve disciples didn't always get it right. Not having to defend the attitudes and behaviors of other Christians grants us the freedom to focus on what it's really all about: Jesus Christ.

Thought for the day: When you talk to someone about Christians, talk about yourself and how Christ has moved in your own life. You are the Christian you know the best.

13. *There's Hope for Us, Yet*
by Theresa Benson

Today's scripture: Romans 7

My Mom's Bible, which I inherited when she died, is probably my most favorite and treasured book. It's an old "hippie" Catholic Bible from 1976, and, amazingly, it was printed right here in Huntington, Indiana. It has pictures of college-age kids from the 70s, with Farrah Fawcett and Dorothy Hamill haircuts. My favorite part was the little set of quotations in the beginning like *"When you want to find out what true love is: 1 Corinthians 13"* or *"When you've been offended: 1 Corinthians 6."*

There's still a bookmark that I snuck into this particular place, right at the page where Romans 7 begins. Sometimes, in the middle of the night, I would steal into the living room, take the Bible off the shelf, and read Romans 7 over and over again because, in the front of the book, it said, *"When you're struggling to do right, and can't quite make it: Romans 7, 8."*

I was nine, I think, when I first found this passage, and I read it over and over until I was 17 and moved away from home. And even though I had my own Bible then, Romans 7 never spoke to me the way it did in my Mom's Bible.

When I was nine, my parents split up, and all the abuse my half-sister — who moved away with my Dad — was getting from my Mom was now all directed toward me, with no other real outlet available for her anger. No matter how I folded the towels, it was wrong; if I got less than a 90% on a test, I was stupid. When the popular girls at school started confiding in me about boys they liked through notes, my Mom found them all, unfolded them, and laid them carefully on top of my bed so there would be no mistaking that she found them, read them, and had a particular opinion about my behavior.

At the same time the psychological and physical abuse was going on at home, I was putting on weight and getting breasts, hips, and zits before everyone else because of steroids I'd been on for asthma. So I got the nickname "Big Butt Benson." Secretly, these girls would share with me their nervousness about boys, school work, or their parents, but they'd pick on me when anyone else was looking.

It was a confusing time — and as children do, I came up with the only answer I could think of to explain what was going on. I decided there was something wrong with me. This passage in my Mom's Bible held out some kind of hope for me. I found empathy with the author — struggling to do right, screwing up, and realizing that following Jesus helps to free him from sin and his sinful ways.

I am so blessed to have found Romans 7 when I was a girl. And in reading now years later, I feel even more blessed to see how much its meaning has changed for me. It still rings true for me, but now I can see it applies to all of us.

Today, when I'm frustrated because I'm not doing what I think God wants me to do, or I screw up in my relationships with others, or my willingness to serve gets weak, I turn to Romans 7 again to remind me that I'm human, and that for thousands of years we've all struggled to get it right — and that, in Jesus, there's hope for me yet.

Thought for the day: In Jesus, there's hope for us — no matter how badly and how often we mess up.

14. *Rescue Me*
by Steve Adams

Today's scripture: Psalm 69:13–15

During my teenage years I felt absolutely trapped in my sexuality. No one could ever find out the terrible secret that I was attracted to boys instead of girls! I had some wonderful family and friends, but I was afraid that, if they knew the real me, they might not respect me anymore. During my first 20 years of life, I learned a bad lesson; if it's a really big problem, then don't talk to anybody about it!

The big enemy that grew in my mind during this struggle was fear. By the time I was in my thirties, I had even developed obsessive compulsive disorder, checking multiple times to see if I had locked the door or performed a task correctly at work. But it's no wonder! Since the onset of puberty, each time I experienced my God-given gift of sexual attraction, my mind would send a message (sometimes verbal, but usually non-verbal) saying, "That was wrong! YOU are wrong! Why aren't you like everybody else?" When I think of how many times I heard that message, I see how my pattern of fear was inevitable.

However, God had other plans for me! Through years of being in different Christian communities, I got some practice in talking to others about uncomfortable subjects that needed to be addressed. A very gifted and patient therapist helped along the way, too, often while I struggled for five minutes trying to get the words out! Now I am usually able to speak to whomever I need to about difficult issues. It's not easy, but God has helped me to retrain my mind.

I remember seeing the first *Rocky* movie when I was a young Christian, and really identifying with the theme of victorious deliverance. Rocky worked hard, fell short, made mistakes, but always persevered. I hope that's how we can be as Christians with whatever blocks us from God. For, even if we are never delivered from some of our prisons in this life, we know that, when we see our Lord Jesus Christ face to face, we will experience complete deliverance in the presence of God and our loved ones!

Thought for the day: Lord, thank you that you can give me the courage to talk to whomever I need to about any difficult issue that needs to be addressed. Thank you that I can learn to love others in this way.

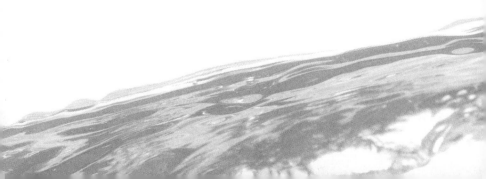

15. *Worry, Worry, Worry!*
by Robert Ferguson

Today's scripture: Philippians 4:6–7

It seems all we can do these days is worry. How are we going to pay this bill? Who is going to pick up the kids? What will I do if I or someone in my family gets sick? Everywhere we turn there's a new fear, concern, or trouble. With the state of the world today, it's easy to get caught up in national security fears, gasoline price fears, and fear of Donald Trump's hair! If we aren't careful, we could spend every waking hour of every day worrying about or being afraid of something.

Be encouraged! In today's reading, Paul encourages us to stop needless worrying and deliver our prayers of praise and petition directly to the heart of God. We are reminded that is it good to know that in these uncertain and ever-changing times God remains un-changed. It really doesn't matter what the circumstance or situation is — God is and always will be in control.

Be thankful! Paul also reminds us to submit our prayers to God with thanksgiving. We always have to thank God for grace and

mercy. I have often been fond of saying, "God, I don't care if you never do another thing for me. You have been good to me thus far." Chief among our requests is that God's will be done. It seems very popular today to ask God to fill our wish lists — and certainly we are encouraged throughout the scriptures to take all of our concerns to the Lord in prayer. However, is there anything wrong with just saying "thank you" for one more day?

Be peaceful! Finally, our text for today reminds us that when we act on our faith and submit our prayers with thanksgiving that our hearts and minds will be guarded by the peace of God, a peace that comes from knowing that God is interested in us and the things that happen to us. Because we have displayed an interest in what God thinks, we can begin to be reconciled, receive redemption, and experience the peace of God.

Thought for the day: If I'm full of worry, does that leave any room for the peace of Christ?

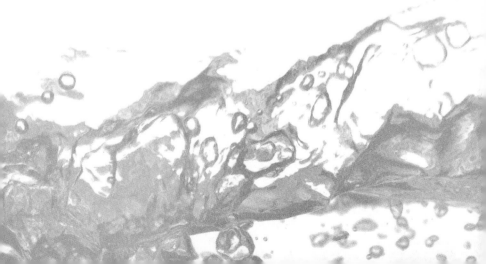

16. Who's Your Daddy?
by Morgan Stewart

Today's scripture: Ephesians 5:1–2

In a souvenir shop over summer vacation, a lovely cross-stitched plaque caught my eye. It read: *A mother's children are portraits of herself.*

As an adoptive mother, I felt a twinge of pain as I gazed at my young twins. In their faces, I see strong resemblances to the strawberry blonde young woman I met some eight and a half years ago. Fully freckled and towering above me in height, she is their birth mother. Can it be that my girls are actually absent of my own reflection?

Many things came to mind about my own mixed bag of genetic "roots." I am an adoptive parent, but also an adoptive child. As an adult, I can easily see that I carry traits of both my biological parent and my adoptive parent.

I'm sure it's the same way with my daughters. While their impish faces sport freckles and dimples from another source, my Christian values, sunny disposition, and even quirky sense of humor reside there as well. Like me, they seem to be a blend of those who birthed them and those who raised them.

It's similar for all Christians. While many of us sport our biological parents' facial features, we are just as likely to bear some marks of our heavenly Parent's nature — perhaps God's love, generosity, kindness, joy, or peace.

Thought for the day: Celebrate the blessing of being related to our heavenly Parent. As God's children, we are indeed a portrait of our Creator.

17. Fear Not!
by Tommy Chittenden

Today's scripture: Isaiah 43:1–7

In scripture the command, "fear not," appears 65 times and another 200 times in different variations — i.e. "do not fear." Of everything commanded by God, the prophets, the apostles, angels, and others, "fear not" might be the command that shows up most often.

This communicates at least two very important things. First, fear just might be the most common human condition. And, second, it is the reaction to life that is least warranted for a follower of Christ.

So what is it you fear? Perhaps a financial setback leading you to feel less secure? Perhaps anxiety about how your children are going to "turn out" and survive in this scary world? Could it be a disease that has compromised your body or that of a loved one? Or maybe your fear is just some indefinite aching anxiety about your own future.

Whatever it is, the amazing words in today's scripture provide the resolution for any fear or anxiety. The question is: How much do we really want to have resolution, that peace of mind available to each of us?

Israel's long history of oppression, captivity, and discrimination would seem to warrant a natural inclination to be anxious, to be fearful. Even with all of the wonderful, amazing miracles and

moments of Israel's deliverance by Yahweh, the prophet now delivers (verses 1, 5a, 6b, 7) one of the most beautiful and hopeful messages recorded. Yet it is not a message just for the nation of Israel; as children of God, we feel it resonate in our own hearts too.

> But now thus says the Lord, he who created you, O Jacob, he who formed you, O Israel: Do not fear, for I have redeemed you; I have called you by name, you are mine. . . . Do not fear, for I am with you . . . bring my sons from far away and my daughters from the end of the earth — everyone who is called by my name, whom I created for my glory, whom I formed and made.

Now pay very close attention to verse 4: ". . . you are precious in my sight, and honored, and I love you. . . ."

How is it possible that when we recognize just how valued and loved we are, and when we see the hand of God in our life's journey, we continue to struggle with fear?

The dangers, afflictions, and challenges we face will not destroy us. Instead we will "pass through the waters . . . and walk through that fire" (verse 2). This is what God has said, and God cannot lie.

Thought for the day: Because God has redeemed us, because we are God's — fear not!

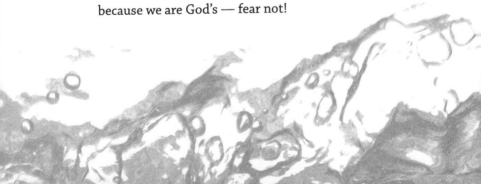

18. A Raging Fire
by Jeff Miner

Today's scripture: James 3:1–12

I really like this passage of scripture. It's tough, but honest. It's like a cold slap in the face that awakens me to a key vulnerability. It's like a good coach who pulls players aside before an important game and sternly warns them to guard against their greatest weakness. That kind of advice is priceless.

Here James reminds us that, regardless of who we are, one of our greatest vulnerabilities will always be our mouths. James says, "Anyone who makes no mistakes in speaking is perfect" (verse 2b). In other words, everybody is going to make mistakes in speaking, because nobody's perfect. So the best we can hope is to control the problem.

Years ago, I was part of a Christian Fellowship Group at the law school I attended. For one of our outreach projects, we decided to invite students from the local school for the blind to share a dinner with us at the law school — an opportunity for them to learn a bit about what it's like to go to law school. As the students arrived and began to take their places, I noticed that some of the folks from our Christian Fellowship Group were clustering together, leaving blind students to themselves. So I made a little announcement, reminding folks to mix and mingle, so everyone could get acquainted.

Afterward, a friend from the Christian Fellowship Group said to me, "Do you realize what you said?"

"What do you mean?"

"When you made that announcement, do you realize what you said?"

I was completely puzzled. "What did I say?"

"You said, 'When you sit down to dinner, make sure one of our normal folks is sitting next to each student.'"

"I didn't say that!" I insisted.

"Yes, you did."

"I wouldn't be that stupid; I couldn't have said that."

"Yes, you did." Then she brought someone over to confirm.

In retrospect, the only thing I can figure is that I meant to say, "Make sure one of us who normally attends our group sits next to each student." But my words came out all wrong. Needless to say, the blind students — accustomed to being seen as abnormal — were very hurt by my words. I have often reflected on that experience and wished I could take back what I said. But I can't.

Once spoken, a word is forever. With that in mind, each one of us should proceed with great caution. Like the Psalmist, we should regularly pray,

> Let the words of my mouth . . . be acceptable to you, O Lord, my rock and my redeemer (Psalm 19:14).

Thought for the day: You are armed with a deadly weapon — your mouth. Don't fire it off carelessly!

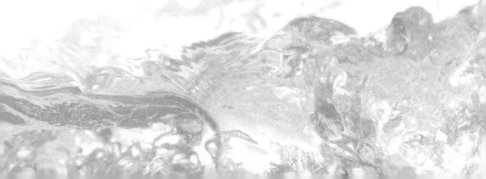

19. *Eating from the Tree*
by Tyler Connoley

Today's scripture: Genesis 3:1–7

Most of us probably think we know this story. God says, "Don't eat the apple." Adam and Eve disobey God and eat the apple — and sin comes into the world. The story has appeared in so many paintings and children's books that it has become part of our subconscious. We know this story even if we weren't raised in the church and never opened a Bible in our lives. However, I'd like us to look at it and try to read it with fresh eyes.

Before I go any farther I should probably say something about *myth,* which is the type of story this is. Being a myth doesn't tell us anything about a story's *factuality,* but it does mean that the people who first told it thought it was true of every human. This is a story that happened, that happens, and that will always happen. As a myth, this passage says as much about us today as it does about Adam and Eve. Just like those earliest humans, each of us has eaten of the Tree of Knowledge of Good and Evil.

Reading the story carefully, what are the consequences of eating from the Tree of Knowledge of Good and Evil? God says if we eat of it, then we will surely die. The serpent says we will be like God, knowing good from evil. I believe both God and the serpent told the truth.

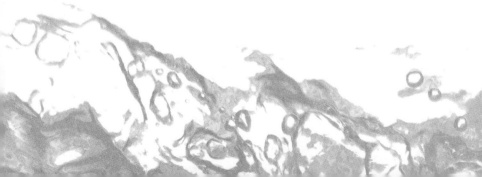

Unlike the rest of God's creations, humans have the ability to know moral good from moral bad. We usually begin to gain this knowledge around the age of four. At that same age, we first realize that we will one day die. So eating from the Tree of Knowledge means that each of us is like God in our ability to know good from evil, and it also means that we know we will die. This causes two profound problems for us.

The first problem is that, while we know good from evil, we don't always do good. Although we're "like God" in our ability to differentiate good from evil, we don't have God's perspective, so even when we think we're doing good, we make mistakes. This can paralyze us when we need to make decisions about what to do.

The second problem is that we fear death. The fear is not always strong, but the fact of our mortality is always with us, just under the surface. Sometimes the realization that we are mortal can paralyze us. We're afraid to do things we know we should, because we don't want to risk death.

I believe Jesus helps us get over these two problems. Tomorrow and the next day, we'll look at how Jesus counteracts the effects of eating from the Tree.

Thought for the day: I know good from evil, and I know I will die. Just like Adam and Eve, I have eaten from the Tree of Knowledge of Good and Evil.

20. *Knowledge of Good and Evil*
by Tyler Connoley

Today's scripture: Luke 6:47–49

Yesterday, we talked about two of the problems that face us as people who have eaten from the Tree of Knowledge of Good and Evil. The first problem is that even though we are "like God" in our ability to know right from wrong, we don't always know what the best thing is to do. Sometimes we simply do bad things, knowing they're bad. But, more often, we try to do good, and it turns out for evil, because our perspective is too small.

In today's passage, Jesus tells us how he can help us with that problem. The earliest disciples gathered around Jesus because they recognized him as a teacher of God's wisdom. In the Gospel of John, we're told they thought of him as God's Word made flesh — Holy Wisdom in human form.

Today, we can read Jesus' teachings and find the same wisdom in them that his earliest followers did. Thanks to the writers of the Gospels, we can be Jesus' disciples and he can be our teacher, even in the 21st century. This is how Jesus helps us with one of the big dilemmas of having eaten from the Tree of Knowledge of Good and Evil.

Instead of being stuck with our own small wisdom, we can build on the foundation of Jesus' teachings. We can become wise people, who build our houses on rock. A house built on rock is more likely to be built well, and the same is true of our lives. If we build our lives on the rock of Christ's teaching, we will more consistently do good instead of evil, and our lives will be sturdier.

I'm not implying that studying Jesus' teachings is the only way to know how to do good more consistently. There are other teachers who teach us right from wrong. The Gospels are only 4 of 66 books in the Bible, and God has given us other wise people to whom we should pay attention. However, listening to Jesus certainly gives us a good foundation to build on.

Thought for the day: You are "like God" in your ability to know good from evil, but are you building on a good foundation so you can make sure you do good instead of evil?

21. *You Shall Surely Die*
by Tyler Connoley

Today's scripture: 1 Corinthians 15:20–23

Yesterday, I presented one way that I believe Jesus helps us get past the problems we face as people who have eaten from the Tree of Knowledge of Good and Evil: Jesus helps us know how to do good more consistently. I also said that Jesus is not unique in his ability to teach us God's wisdom. Today, however, I want to talk about a unique way that Jesus helps us.

Of all the creatures living on the earth, we appear to be the only ones who keep track of time. We are the only ones knowledgeable enough to notice anniversaries and birthdays. When September 11 arrives each year, the pigeons in Central Park don't shudder, but the people do. Our dogs haven't noticed that the oldest dog in the house was only 15 when she died. They don't think, "I'm seven. That's middle age. I may only have a few good years left!" However, we humans have certainly noticed that we're pushing 40.

Death is one of our great dilemmas as people who have eaten from the Tree of Knowledge of Good and Evil. We are all afraid of death, and yet we all have the knowledge that it is inevitable. It is the specter that haunts our days and nights, the end that we all try to avoid, though we know we never will.

This is why Christ's resurrection is such a potent symbol of hope for us, and why Paul saw it as key to the message of Christianity. Christ can free us from our deepest fear.

I don't think it matters whether you believe Jesus rose from the dead with a body that ate and drank (like Luke's account), or whether you believe the risen Christ was a shining Spirit of light (like the one who met Paul on the road to Damascus). What gives me hope is that I know Christ rose from the dead. As Paul says, "But in fact Christ has been raised from the dead, the first fruits of those who have died" (verse 20).

Imagine the hopelessness that must have overcome the earliest disciples after their teacher, the man who brought them God's wisdom, was killed by the powers of evil. After the fact his death seemed inevitable. How could one so good not be overcome by evil? And, knowing this, how could they expect anything else for themselves? The world seemed more doomed than ever, so they went and hid.

Yet all of the earliest testimonies agree that the crucifixion was not the end of Jesus. These men and women who began as completely demoralized people were energized to carry the "good news" to everyone they knew! How is that possible? I believe they were energized by the hope they found in encountering their teacher risen from the dead.

In Jesus, God made it known to them that death is not the end. Whatever evil things humans may do, God will transform them into good. This is the message of hope that overturns what we think we know about good, evil, and death. Resurrection is real, and death is not the end.

Thought for the day: Are you afraid of death? Reread Matthew 28, Luke 24, John 20–21, and Acts 1–2. The earliest disciples were certain of the resurrection, and we can trust the One who raised Jesus from the dead.

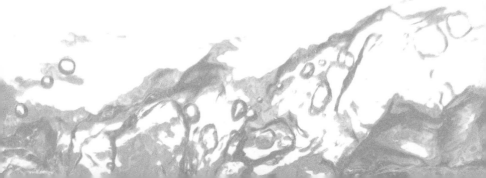

22. *Who's Driving?*
by Pam Beutler

Today's scripture: Matthew 6:25–34

We live in fast times. Food service is never fast enough. Lines never move fast enough for our schedules — whether at the bank, grocery store, movie theater, or in rush hour traffic. Has your partner ever said to you, "We never spend enough time together"? We are exhausted from just "living." Some of us talk about simpler times and fewer responsibilities.

God wants us to enjoy life, to stop and smell the roses or to listen to the rustle of falling leaves on an Indiana autumn day. In our minds, we can come up with more reasons not to relax, more tasks that must be done.

Just for today — take deliberate breaths. Feel yourself taking in a breath and exhaling. Feel your heart beat.

Just for today — turn off the radio or television, pick up a pen, and write a letter to God. Tell God what you're feeling.

Just for today — count your blessings. Worry less about what you don't have, and appreciate what you do.

We make life harder than God intended it to be. God gave us nature to enjoy, not destroy. God gave us our senses to take in the beauty of all creation.

We fret way too much about our bodies. We overfeed them, or underfeed them. We put chemicals into them and food that isn't nourishing — all for the pleasure of it. We rarely use this wonderful mind God gave us to contemplate how easy life could truly be. We can explore our dreams and make them into reality. We can develop our full potential, which would in turn nourish our souls and please God.

God, our Creator, made us perfect. Our souls are in God's image. We are on this earth to enjoy and experience life — not constantly fight it. Our priorities should be to grow our soul, achieving the levels that Jesus showed us are possible on earth; to develop and expand our mind to that higher plane; and to use our bodies as tools, assisting in the other two priorities.

Starting today, show gratitude for your life and the things that you have been given. Slow down — let God drive your life and give your body a rest. You might be surprised where it takes you.

Thought for the day: I'll move to God's rhythm.

23. *Dreams Come True*
by Keith Phillips

Today's scripture: Genesis 50:15–21

I have dreams: dreams of my future, dreams of effecting change in our world, dreams for my children and closest friends, dreams for our church, dreams for the LGBTQ community, dreams of being with someone special. We all have dreams, or I suppose we wouldn't be human.

The story of Joseph is about dreams: the dreams of his eleven brothers' sheaves of grain bowing down to his, and the dream of the sun, moon, and eleven stars bowing down to him. These dreams made his brothers angry, and maybe made Joseph a little arrogant. Still, I'm sure he was cute; you know the type.

The story goes on. The brothers grab Joseph and sell him into slavery. Then Joseph is falsely accused of seducing his master's wife, and he's thrown into an Egyptian prison. Then, after interpreting a dream, Joseph becomes Pharaoh's right-hand man, saves the country during a famine, and feeds his brothers who have come groveling to him (although they don't know it's him). His whole family moves to Egypt, but their father, Jacob, dies. And now the brothers think that Joseph might seek revenge. Strange thing about guilt: we do wrong, and it produces fear and anxiety.

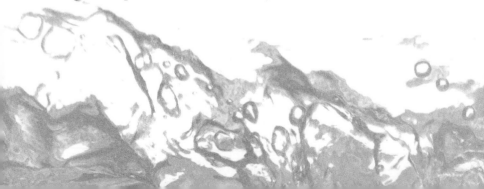

However, Joseph says, "You planned evil against me but God used those same plans for my good . . ." (verse 20; *The Message*). God's purposes are working themselves out, even through the worst we can imagine. That's grace, triumphing over evil.

But it's not "cheap grace" (a term used by Dietrich Bonhoeffer, martyred by the Nazis). Grace is not leaving everything in God's hands and doing nothing, but rather grace is recognizing that God has no hands but ours. God's plans shall triumph, but we will have fought a battle.

Joseph's dreams came true: his brothers did bow before him. God worked through some pretty awful stuff to do that. But the dream of the eleven brothers came true as well: "life for many people" (verse 20; *The Message*). That's grace, triumphing over sin and guilt, too.

I pray that my dreams are the dreams of God for me. And I pray that I have the faith and the courage to face whatever battles are before me so that they shall come true.

> **Thought for the day:** What are your dreams? Do they align with the will of God for you? Are you allowing yourself to be used by God so that these dreams shall come true?

24. *Teach Me, Lord!*
by Steve Adams

Today's scripture: Isaiah 43:1–7

When I was twelve years old, my grandmother told me, "When I was 16, I thought I knew everything there was to know! I thought I was so smart!" My immediate thought (which I didn't verbalize) was "When you're 16, you do know just about everything, don't you?" By the time I eventually did turn 16, there was, of course, still so much I didn't know! Then I looked forward to college as the time when I'd be filled with all knowledge — but no, it didn't happen! After that, I thought learning about the Bible and becoming a committed Christian would do the trick. As much as that helped, I still wasn't there by a long shot. Later I thought maybe retirement would give me the time to "learn it all."

I've come to the realization that there will be important things I'll need to learn every day for the rest of my life, even if I live to be 100, and even then, my knowledge will only be partial. I think this is true even for the most enlightened among us. It's not a weak faith that realizes there's a lot more to learn, but a strong one.

This directly relates to Israel as described by Isaiah. If anyone should be wise, it should be God's chosen people, right? It would have been easy for them to think they knew more than everybody else. Well, God had a different assessment! "Who is blind but my servant, or deaf like my messenger whom I send? . . . He sees many things, but does not observe them; his ears are open, but he does not hear" (42:19a and 20). Israel had been missing it, off the mark, falling far short of the quality of life God wanted for them.

However, I think something powerfully life-changing took place in the heart of the people of Israel which enabled them to receive the sterling promises made in today's scripture. They came to realize that they not only didn't know it all, but needed to orient their entire souls to God in a deeper, more earnest way than they ever had before. They realized they needed to repent. And they did! As a result, they hungered for God's blessings to reach others, not just themselves. "I have taken you by the hand and kept you. . . to open the eyes that are blind, to bring out the prisoners from the dungeon" (Isaiah 42:6b, 7b).

Thought for the day: Lord, I hunger to learn more of your precious knowledge and wisdom! Help me never to be complacent with what I now know, and always eager to learn the lessons that you want to teach me and that I so desperately need to learn.

25. Do You Want to Be Healed?
by Christen Peters

Today's scripture: John 5:1–15

The many times I've heard this story told, or have read it, I've seen it as an example of Jesus throwing out rabbinic emphasis on the law in favor of doing the greater good. In doing so, Jesus touched off the conflict that would lead to his crucifixion.

I've always wondered, though, why Jesus singled out this person. This man has been paralyzed for 38 years, which must have been the vast majority of his life. Because of his handicap, he probably had never married. I can only surmise that it was members of his extended family who delivered him to the pool each day. Once they'd gotten him there, they went about their daily lives. They probably hoped like heck that he'd manage to make it into the pool so that they didn't have to deal with having such an outcast in their family anymore.

This man had begun to feel so hopeless that, when Jesus asked him if he wanted to be healed, the man failed to even recognize Jesus' offer of wholeness. He merely recounted the reason why he hadn't gotten better already. In spite of it all, Jesus told him to gather his mat and go — as if he'd been whole all the while and only needed someone to tell him so.

Does this sound even a little familiar? How many times have you heard of families depositing gay men and women on the doorsteps of religion, hoping that they'll be "cured"? Have you ever felt like an outcast in your family, school, neighborhood, city, and country? Have you ever cried in the night to be healed of this thing that seems to have separated you from the rest of the world and from God? How many times have you failed to recognize that you are already whole — you need only pick up your mat and go!

Don't let yourself be thrown by verse 14. Doesn't it seem unreasonable that Jesus considered the man to have been paralyzed because of some sin he had committed? I think the sin Jesus is talking about here is a loss of faith or a failure to see the nearness of God in all things and at all times. We talk often about how people come to Christ all gung-ho, then seem to fade away. I think Jesus is warning this man not to fall away from God again. And I think we would do well to heed the same warning.

Thought for the day: What is keeping me from seeing the nearness of God, and my own wholeness in God?

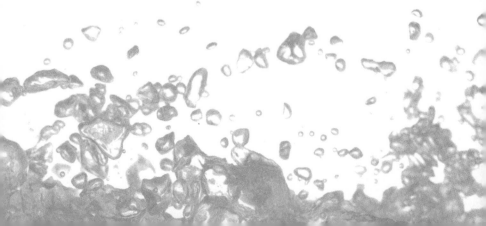

26. *It's Not Fair!*
by Brent Walsh

Today's scripture: Romans 14:1–4

When I was in junior high school, my sister Joyce and I had a part-time job delivering a weekly newspaper. Every Wednesday morning we would drag ourselves out of bed at 4:30 to roll newspapers until our fingers were black from the ink. Once they were rolled and fastened with rubber bands, we would walk the route together, delivering a paper to each house in our neighborhood.

The work was fun for the first two weeks, but then the novelty wore off and I struggled to get out of bed so early. I grumbled about the chill of the mornings, the ache in my legs, the ink on my hands, and the monotony of the route.

When my first paycheck came, somehow my ill feelings about the job were replaced with excitement at having earned my very own money! That check represented hard work and accomplishment, and I couldn't wait to find something at the store on which to spend my money! My father, however, had a different idea.

"I want you to learn about saving money," he said. "When you've saved at least a hundred dollars, then we can talk about what you want from the store."

"But it's my money! I earned it! I worked hard for it! Why can't I spend it the way I want to?" I argued, but to no avail. The rule was set, and there was nothing I could do to convince my father otherwise.

Several years later, my younger brother, David, thought of a brilliant way to earn money. He bought soda and candy bars, put them in a cooler, and took them around on his bike to all the construction sites in our neighborhood. The workers would buy his ice-cold soda and candy, providing David with a nice profit. When I asked my brother about his savings account, he said he didn't have one.

"How did you get around Dad's rule?" I asked, wondering at the cleverness of my sibling. "What rule?" he asked. "The rule that we have to put all our earnings into a savings account," I answered. But my brother had never heard of such a rule.

I was confused. How could my dad have overlooked such a thing? I went to him and inquired about his forgetfulness. He told me that the rule about saving money didn't apply to David.

"That is so unfair!" I said, in shock. "Don't you think that when you make a rule, it should apply to everyone?"

"David doesn't have a problem with spending money," my father explained. "He thinks about the long-term. I don't need to make that rule for him because he doesn't need to learn what I was trying to teach you."

When I look back on that and other times in which rules only applied to one or two members of the family, I feel that I can get a better grasp on understanding God. If it seems that others can "get away" with things we never can, we might jump to the conclusion that God is inconsistent and unfair.

But when we find ourselves there, we should look a bit deeper. Maybe that person is learning different lessons than we are. Let's not judge them according to the rules we follow. God will work in the life of each person differently, so let's spend our time learning — rather than throwing tantrums and saying, "It's not fair!"

Thought for the day: It's not fair? Maybe not. But maybe it's what God knows I need.

27. For You, Theophilus
by Tyler Connoley

Today's scripture: Luke 1:1–4

Traditionally, the words in today's passage are said to have been written by Luke, the beloved physician mentioned in Colossians 4:14. However, we will never know the actual identity of the author, because his name has been lost to history. He never mentions his own name in the book itself, only that he is writing "for you, most excellent Theophilus."

Most Christians, of course, view all the Gospels as part of the Word of God — Holy Scripture. Odd as it may seem, this fact used to distance me from the texts of the Gospels. I felt like I needed to approach them with special reverence, like a priest entering the Holy of Holies. I took them too seriously to take them seriously.

Then, one day, as I read the first few sentences of the Gospel of Luke, I really listened to what this author was saying: "I too decided, after investigating everything carefully from the very first, to write an orderly account for you" (verse 3).

This wasn't someone setting out to write Scripture, like a prophet channeling God. He was an early follower of Jesus, who had tried to discern what actually happened when Jesus was walking the earth, and then wrote down what he'd learned. He was writing a history, as best he could, having "investigated everything carefully." He was also attempting to tell "the truth concerning the things about which you have been instructed" (verse 4).

With this in mind, I reread the Gospel of Luke as a history. Like Theophilus — which means "lover of God" — I was someone who wanted to be a disciple of Jesus, and this was a careful accounting of what Jesus said and did. Instead of approaching the text with reverence and awe, I approached it with interest and curiosity. How did Jesus live? What did Jesus say? How might his teaching apply to me?

The result was a complete reorientation of my life. For me, it was the beginning of being able to finally say, "Jesus is Lord of my life," and mean it.

> **Thought for the day:** Are you a lover of God? Then Luke was written for you, "so that you may know the truth concerning the things about which you have been instructed." This is a careful history written so you, Theophilus, might know Jesus better.

28. *Hope in the Lord*
by Keith Phillips

Today's scripture: Psalm 131

Recently I was reading to a dementia patient from Romans 8 (the King James Version, of course, is what dementia patients like best), eager to get to the part about nothing separating us from the love of God; but I ran across verse 24, which begins: "for we are saved by hope." All of a sudden, bells went off. What would Martin Luther say? Every evangelical Christian knows that we are saved by grace through faith (Ephesians 2:8).

I then realized, maybe for the first time, that hope and faith are very closely related. It struck me how, especially in times like these, hope is a function of faith. It is precisely because I have faith, because I completely trust God and God's unconditional love for me, that I can have the hope that everything is all right, everything will be all right, just as, when I look back, everything has been all right. How remarkable to be led to this learning by a dementia patient. God can use any of us!

The Psalmist encourages God's people to hope, in verse 3. In verses 1 and 2, the Psalmist describes himself and why it is that he can hope. Humility is obviously the key. It is so easy to think that I have to be in control of everything, that I should be in charge of my own destiny. The truth is that there's mighty little, beyond myself, that I can truly control. This is where I know I must trust God. God is sovereign. God's loving power is phenomenal; I've seen it at work in my life in ways that are beyond comprehension. How is it that I, an extraordinary sinner, have been so blessed?

I've found that true humility leads to contentment, the kind of contentment and satisfaction that weaned babies have lying upon their mother's breasts. What a beautiful picture of our relationship with God, too! No longer whining and harassing God to take care of us; we have grown and are weaned from that kind of relationship. Yet we know that God will care for us. In quiet contentment, with a humble, proper sense of self, we wait with hope and faith for what God will do next. We are ready for what the future has in store for us.

Thought for the day: Mother God, you have fed me from infancy. You have provided for all my needs. I have faith that you will always do that. Because of you, I can hope. Amen.

29. *The Tapping Paw of Assurance*
by Mark Shoup

Today's scripture: Psalm 131

I am the proud father of a very co-dependant schnauzer.

Ausker is a very easy-going, lovable dog as long as I am in physical contact with him. He will sit next to me while I watch television, lie at my feet while I use the computer, and lie alongside of me when I sleep. In fact, while he is doing one of these three things, he will ignore the puppy chewing on his ears, remain oblivious to the ball you throw for him, and bat not an eye at the barking dogs on the television screen.

However, should it suddenly occur to him that he is not in actual physical contact with me, he will immediately set about tapping my arm with his paw. It's as if he is saying "Daddy, have you forgotten about me? Did you forget that I was here? Please give me some kind of sign that you haven't forgotten about me!" And once the situation has deteriorated to the paw-tapping stage, nothing but excessive amounts of petting will console his little broken heart and reassure him that I really do care and always will.

It reminds me of a few lines from A. A. Milne's *Winnie the Pooh* that I read when I was a kid:

Piglet sidled up to Pooh from behind. "Pooh!" he whispered.
"Yes, Piglet?"
"Nothing," said Piglet, taking Pooh's paw. "I just wanted to be sure of you."

I think Piglet and Ausker understand what David expresses in today's psalm — but so few of us really get it. That is, that God is most pleased with us when we are focused solely on God, when there is so much God in our view that we can't see anything else, when there is so much God on our minds that we can't think about anything else.

Thought for the day: The next time life seems overwhelming to me, I think I'm going to take a page out of my schnauzer's book and start tapping God's arm with my paw.

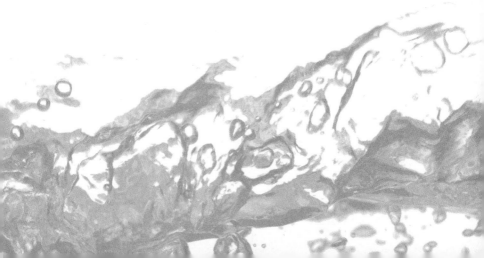

30. *A New Perspective*
by Steve Adams

Today's scripture: Romans 12:12

These three short commands have been a source of great strength and inspiration to me for many years. When the pressure of life is on, they put wings to my soul! I'd like to tell you why.

Rejoice in hope . . . Have you ever thought about how rejoicing in something enables you to transcend circumstances? When I was trying to endure a painful and discouraging job, with no prospects for change, each day I would struggle to overcome futile and frustrating feelings that would well up inside. However, I remember one day when conditions were as bleak as usual, yet I was hardly able to contain the joy I felt! What had happened? I was rejoicing! You see, I had just met the love of my life. Suddenly, it was much easier to put the work situation in proper perspective!

What does it mean to rejoice in hope? Our great hope is living with our Lord Jesus Christ for eternity in his kingdom. This hope is not a wish, like when we say, "I hope it's a nice day on Saturday." No, it's a certainty! God has promised and will deliver! Doesn't it arouse your deepest longing to think of living in God's kingdom, with no more suffering, injustice, or death? In the coming age we'll no longer have to struggle with evil from others or with our own sinful

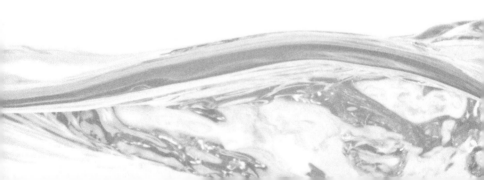

natures! When this hope becomes real to us, it will improve our perspective more than falling in love!

Be patient in suffering . . . If I have patience, then I will continue on the path God has given me, even if I have to endure hardship. In other words, I won't quit! Luke 8:15 speaks of those who "bring forth fruit with patience" (King James Version). The New International Version translates this same phrase as "by persevering produce a crop." So those who are patient persevere in a godly path through the long, hard days as well as the bright, sunny ones.

Persevere in prayer . . . Several years ago I prayed with others from a prayer list during the Pizza and Prayer meeting at church. Suddenly I felt inspired to say, "We need to pray for people who aren't on this list, too." Less than six months later, several people we knew from church who weren't on the list had severe life crises which had begun before that prayer meeting. Even though I often fall short in how much I pray, this nevertheless taught me that it is critical we pray even for those who appear to be doing well. A comprehensive prayer list is great, but there is so much unknown and downright mysterious in life; it is impossible to know every critical need.

On the other hand, your prayers may help others break through into a wonderful new realm that God has prepared for them. Just think, maybe it's your prayer that gets them through! Other types of prayer, like conversing with and giving thanks to God, are also invaluable so that we can pour our hearts out to God, hear God's wisdom, and give thanks for the good things.

Thought for the day: Today I will rejoice in eternal life with Jesus Christ, be patient in the hard times, and pray earnestly and joyfully!

31. *Cleaning Cobwebs from My Mind*
by David Zier

Today's scripture: Philippians 4:8

I hate it when I let myself get distracted by stuff that takes away my focus and clutters up my mind. Not long ago, I was feeling that someone was being nice to me because of a sense of obligation, but basically ignoring me otherwise. No matter what I did or said, it was never good enough. Work I did was never passed on, my ideas were dismissed and belittled, and no matter what I was trying to do, it was ignored.

When all of this was happening, my mind was occupied with thoughts of the things I would like to say — and how that would hurt this other person. Of course I never said anything, so the other person was spared and never hurt. I thought I was being righteous because I never did anything — I just thought about it. So there was no harm done. Right?

When I read this passage in Philippians, it makes me realize that when I fill my mind with this stuff, I may not be hurting the other person, but I am hurting myself! If I waste my time and brain-power with these thoughts, it takes my mind off the honorable, just, commendable, and praiseworthy things I could be thinking about.

I can take this even further and look back at the times I let my mind get preoccupied with all kinds of negative stuff. When I dwell on discouragement, when I'm consumed with selfish motives, when I think about people who have hurt me and what I would like to do or say to them — it is amazing how much time I spend on junk! This stuff provides me no benefit, and takes up time and space in my mind where I could be dwelling on the good things, on righteous, pure, and just things.

Yes, I know our minds wander and can think multiple things at once, especially my multitasking mind. I may never completely conquer those thoughts that have plagued me over and over, but I can be more deliberate. If I allow myself to focus more on what is just, right, and worthy of praise, then this will become more of me, who I am, and how I act. If I allow myself to fill my mind with junk, how will this manifest in my behavior? That thought is scary!

Focusing on the praiseworthy, honorable, just, pleasing, and pure things of God will also encourage me during down times, so that I will then focus less on the things that bring me down.

Thought for the day: Am I focusing my thoughts on the right things?

32. *Waiting for God Knows What*
by David Squire

Today's scripture: Isaiah 40:28–31

A few months ago, our pastor wrote about finding a favorite scripture and "growing into" it. This passage is one I've been growing into — even when I didn't know that's what I was doing.

I grew up in a Christian home. My parents (who have been married 49 years) sacrificed to send all six of their children to a Christian school, where we had Bible classes every day and chapel three times a week. I was a good kid — and pretty sure I was heading on the right path, spiritually speaking.

But about six months after I graduated from that Christian high school, my kidneys failed. Something like that can really throw a monkey wrench in your plans — and make you have questions about your faith. Why would God let something like this happen? I was angry, confused, and scared.

I probably prayed more in the first six months after my kidneys failed than I had in all the chapel services of the previous six years. I found several passages of scripture that gave me hope. Most of them were promises of healing — and I grasped at them and claimed that God would give me physical healing, too.

But then there was this one, Isaiah 40:31. At first I thought it was telling me that I just needed to wait on God for the renewal of my physical strength. But God was up to something else.

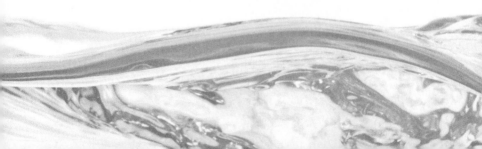

I waited — thinking that a miracle was just around the corner. But in all this "down" time, with study and prayer, I was drawing closer to God. (Funny how that can happen, huh?) My *body* wasn't renewing its strength (dialysis really leaves a body dragging, let me tell you) but my *soul* was starting to learn what it meant to "run and not be weary, walk and not faint."

It's fascinating to me how often God has to tell us to cool our jets. Even in the scripture we named this devotional resource after (Psalm 46:10, another of my favorites), God starts by telling us, "Be still . . ." It's like God sometimes wants to say, "Shut up! Sit down! Stop running around like a crazy person, and just listen!"

A successful transplant a few years later helped the body to catch up to the soul. But this little "detour" I went through helped me to see a few things. My life really does run on God's timetable — and I can either understand that and go with the flow, or I can live with the illusion that I set my own agenda and wonder why I'm always fighting the current. While I thought I was waiting for my body to be made strong again, God wanted to work on my heart — and that's vastly more important. "Those who wait for the Lord shall renew their strength."

Thought for the day: Being still — waiting — is a holy act.

33. *Practice Makes Perfect*
by Julie Walsh

Today's scripture: 1 Timothy 4:7–16

"A music major's homework is never finished," I used to whine in college. "Those pharmacy majors may have a six-year program, but at least when their science test is over, they are through, unlike our daily playing routine." I spent many nights practicing until all hours of the morning — especially toward the end of the semester when we had our playing proficiencies.

I literally shed blood (with my calloused fingers adjusting to a four-mallet percussion grip), sweat (would they ever turn that air conditioning on to compensate for the 90-degree heat?), and tears. It took motivation, which on many days I just didn't have, to drag myself to the practice room. Some of the toughest sessions contained mistake after mistake, resulting in a feeling of failure and inadequacy deep inside.

In today's reading, I realize that my spiritual journey is no different than my musical one. Paul dwells upon a theme in this passage

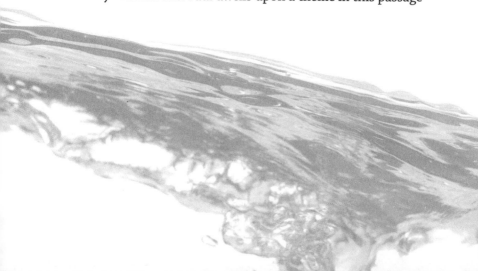

that he sums up with two words in verse 7: "Train yourself." Simply put, he is saying that living a flawless, optimistic, spirit-filled life is not going to come naturally. It will take daily practice.

Training yourself spiritually is much like practicing an instrument, singing, playing a sport, engaging in a hobby, or advancing in a career. You will always have to work consciously and intentionally to improve. In addition, it takes a special willingness to make yourself vulnerable to mistakes and failures along the way. The key is to "put these things into practice . . . so that all may see your progress" (verse 15).

> **Thought for the day:** God, please make me always aware that I'm in training, learning to be more like Jesus. Please give me patience too, Lord, as I remember that others around me are also in training.

34. *Revising History*
by Tyler Connoley

Today's scripture: Psalm 34:4–10

Recently, a friend's 80-pound dog, Henry, almost succeeded in killing my little 11-pound Lucia. We were walking together, and the dogs were playing, when Henry suddenly lost his mind and decided that Lucia was prey instead of playmate. At one point, as Henry's owner and I were struggling to pry his jaws apart, I thought I saw little Lucia die. (She had passed out because he'd closed her windpipe with his bite.) Later, on the way to the vet, Lucia began to gasp for breath, and I again thought she would die in my lap before I could get help.

Lucia is expected to fully recover — no major arteries or vital organs were injured, just lots of bruises and lacerations — but I've found myself unable to get the images from that morning out of my head. One night, as I was lying in bed, unable to sleep because every time I closed my eyes I saw images from that horrible event, I remembered the promise of Psalm 34, that God is always with me and God's angels encamp around me. I felt God tell me to re-imagine the images from that morning.

So I went back in my mind, and I pictured God's light around my friend and me as we struggled with Henry for Lucia's life. I pictured angels holding our hands as we pried at Henry's teeth. I saw God's

hand reaching down into Henry's mind and releasing him from the instinct that had overtaken him, and allowing him to let go of Lucia long enough for us to get her away to safety.

One of the images I can't get out of my mind is of me running to the car, with Lucia in my arms. Now, when I picture that scene, I see the angels that were running right beside me as I whispered my deepest desire, "Lucia, you're going to be okay. Oh God! You're going to be okay, little girl."

I'll never know how God and the angels actually intervened that morning. However, when I choose to picture them within those scenes that haunt my memory, I find Psalm 34:4 is fulfilled — God relieves me from my fears. I can face the next walk with Lucia, the next interaction with a big dog, with more confidence and less fear. With the Psalmist, I can say, "Happy are those who take refuge in [God]" (verse 8b).

Thought for the day: What traumatic images haunt you? Can you allow yourself to revisit those images, and see God and the angels encamped around you? You may not ever know how God was with you in that situation, but you can trust God was.

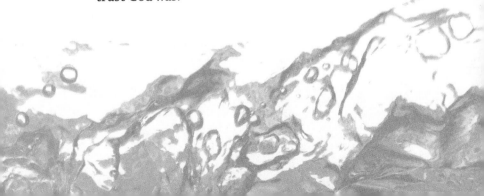

35. *Last Days*
by David Zier

Today's scripture: 2 Timothy 3:1–17

Ever watch the show *Jack Van Impe Presents?* He has been on TV for years. Van Impe analyzes the day's events, showing how they align with scripture. He always emphasizes that the end times are here, or very near. He has been preaching this message as long as I can remember, which means the end times are always here, or near.

Today's scripture tells us what will happen to us in the last days. I can see this scripture in a couple of different ways. Paul tells us to be steadfast in our discipleship journey, and concludes, "so that everyone who belongs to God may be proficient, equipped for every good work" (verse 17). When I read 2 Timothy 3, I don't think Paul is telling us to focus on the end of the world, but to live a life in stead-fast relationship with God. This should be our focus.

As I read this scripture during my own prayer time, I also see the "last days" as a warning of what can happen when I start to stray from God. These could be my "last days" of peace, or my "last days" of living a life of love and joy as God intended. When we become reckless, deceitful, ungrateful, inhuman, lovers of money, arrogant, haters of good, or slanderers, this takes us away from God, and it may seem like we are trapped in our own "last days."

The next time I flip through the channels and see another episode of Jack Van Impe or read of another revelation story, will I look at it as another prophecy of the "end" like many others that seem to drag on and on, or will I examine myself and pray for discernment about how I am living, and ask, "Am I living my last days?"

Thought for the day: Am I living in my "last days"? How can I live a more purposeful, steadfast life for God?

36. *Sarcasm Isn't a Spiritual Gift?!*
by Mark Shoup

Today's scripture: 1 Corinthians 12:4–13

When I was in a discipleship class at our church and learned that we were going to get to take a test to determine what our spiritual gifts might be, I could hardly contain my excitement. I have always enjoyed taking quizzes to find out about my personality or preferences, and I was certain this test would tell me I had the gift of healing or prophecy, or something else of equal flash and excitement.

But once I took the test and the results were analyzed, I didn't have any of those flashy gifts at all. In fact, one of my gifts I had never even heard of, and the one in which I clearly most excel, *sarcasm*, wasn't even on the list! I would be lying if I said that I wasn't a little bit disappointed.

But my teachers were wise and kept stressing the words of 1 Corinthians 12 to us, that it is necessary for us each to have different gifts to make the Church work as it should. Just like a body wouldn't work very well if you had ears for arms and legs, the Church wouldn't work well if the only gift anybody had was the gift of prophecy.

Not long after, I came to the realization that God really wanted me to embrace my spiritual gifts and, in particular, the one on which I had scored highest.

This came at a time when I was out of work on disability with a broken back, and it would have made perfect sense to hold off until I was in a better situation before taking the next step. But, for whatever reason, I didn't, and I began to use my gift in whatever ways I could. Even though my efforts were minor at first, a strange thing began to happen. I could see my gift actually having an impact on the Church, and at the same time I could begin to see my gift growing!

It really didn't matter that I didn't have one of the flashy gifts, because being able to see my gift helping the church ended up being more satisfying than I would have ever thought.

Thought for the day: What are my spiritual gifts, and how can I use them to do my part in the church?

37. *Welcome to the Kingdom of God!*
by Steve Adams

Today's scripture: Matthew 5:1–10; Philippians 2:14–15

I always looked forward to the Saturdays I'd go to Pat's apartment to clean for her. She had severe, life-threatening heart and lung problems, along with other ailments that often prevented her from getting a good night's rest. Even though her apartment complex was in a nice neighborhood, it had fallen into a state of filthy disrepair. The entry hall leading to her door was so dirty the carpet was mostly black, even though it had originally been green, and it was usually littered with paper and other trash.

Inside her door was a completely different world, though. A loving, healing atmosphere greeted me as soon as I walked in. Pat would usually be sitting on her sofa, truly enjoying the day. Unusual, healing scents such as jasmine or eucalyptus rose from small fountains, along with the soothing sound of gently flowing water. Her apartment was a place where God ruled. She was always interested in how I was doing, which caused me to enjoy sharing what was going on in my life. Likewise, I always wanted to know how she was doing, and hear her tell me about the latest, often new and unusual, thing she had discovered.

The best part was talking to her while I cleaned. We would spontaneously get into Christian conversations about the challenges and beauty of life. Pat didn't spend much time even mentioning the deplorable conditions outside her door, because she couldn't control that. She focused on the things she could control, with help from her Lord Jesus Christ. In the mornings, while she was still in bed, Pat would raise her arms in praise to God and say, "I love you; I thank you; I praise you!" She amazingly held onto that attitude throughout the day, despite the pain and suffering her illnesses caused.

I'm sure Pat was often deeply dissatisfied with her health and her apartment building. However, she didn't allow grief and regret to pull her down. Instead, she was able to respond to disappointment with increased motivation to make her life more godly. This freed her mind to be open to what God wanted to tell her, and it was amazing to see the fresh and resourceful ideas she would come up with that made her life fun. And she would always credit God's goodness and love as the origin of her new-found blessings. The bottom line was that she knew God would deliver her from what seemed to be hopeless circumstances, either in this life or the next.

Thank you, Lord, for my friend, Pat. Even though she isn't here anymore to brighten up the world, I thank you she is one of your shining lights in Heaven, giving testimony to your goodness and glory.

Thought for the day: Who has brought Jesus alive to you? Take a few minutes to remember, and thank God for them.

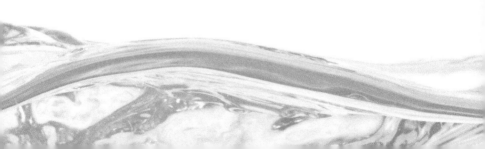

38. *Special Delivery*
by Ben Lamb

Today's scripture: Matthew 14:22–33

I used to think, "Now, why in the world did Jesus go and scare his poor little disciples like that? Anybody would know they'd be frightened half to death to see someone strolling along on top of the water during a raging sea storm."

But after reading it more recently, some things have dawned on me. (It's also amazing what seems to "dawn" on me when I preface my reading of scripture with a prayer asking for God's blessing for the purpose of bringing glory to the Holy Trinity. In earlier times, my reading was sincere enough, but I used to leave out the prayer beforehand.)

An Internet search turned up some facts about the Sea of Galilee, which lies in a basin below sea level. The body of water is 13 miles long, 7 miles wide, and only 150 feet deep at its lowest point. This usually peaceful place can rapidly become violently stormy. Winds can batter the waters from several directions, creating dangerous conditions that become deadly. The resulting waves (as high as 10 feet) literally overcome fishing vessels. Hmmm . . . I'm seeing some allegorical parallels between the Sea of Galilee and everyday life. It sounds as though today's reading is fitting for both the 1st and 21st centuries!

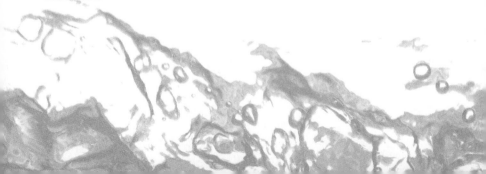

Jesus knew exactly what the occupants of the boat needed: the type of peace that only he could bring. How best could Jesus do that in physical form? There was more than one way, of course. Materialize out of nowhere? That might really have scared them! Calling out to them from the sky? Because it was storming, Jesus would have had to yell quite loudly; hardly a way to comfort anyone, I think.

Calmly walking toward the disciples as a familiar person whom they'd seen hundreds of times already was perfectly logical. When you yourself are feeling stressed, isn't it a pleasure to see a friend if you're at the shopping mall or standing on a sidewalk? Because Jesus was capable of being anywhere, why shouldn't he have walked on over to where his troubled friends were? Some H2O was no insurmountable problem for him.

I can be like Peter sometimes. God makes something perfectly clear to me, but I still doubtingly say, "Is it really you?" or "You want me to do what?" Yet God never gives up on me, thank . . . um . . . God. What a comfort that is. It's not surprising that another name for the Holy Spirit (the one Jesus sent to earth following his ascension back to heaven) is the Great Comforter.

Thought for the day: What a creative God we have! When comforting us, God uses a cornucopia of ways. It's exciting to be open to all sorts of wonderful possibilities!

39. *Consider the Lilies*
by Morgan Stewart

Today's scripture: Luke 12:22–32

These are the very words of Jesus Christ as he teaches his followers about freeing themselves from the worries of this world. Note the things Bible folks were presumably worrying about — food, clothes, income, financial security.

As a reformed chronic worrier, I smiled when I read this on an outdoor sign: Worry is like a rocking chair — it keeps you occupied, but gets you nowhere. These days, my two-fold antidote for worry is this:

Accept the things you cannot change, and
Pray about the rest.

From the stock market to our sexual orientation to a loved one's serious illness, worrying about things we cannot change is futile. It was my close friend Pat who taught me this first principle. When her newborn son was born with a congenital heart defect requiring open-heart surgery, I asked, "Aren't you worried about your baby's health?" But she was adamant. "My son was not born as healthy as we would have liked, but worrying won't change that. I'm using my energy to see that he gets the best surgeon and after-care available." Now that's the way to stay occupied!

Worry is often a character trait of those obsessed with control, and my friend Sheila is typical. As layoff rumors circulated around the water cooler, she worried about losing her job at a local bank. When she expressed concern over the situation, I inquired, "How long have you been praying about this?"

She answered, "My coworkers in the lunch room think layoffs will come after the first of the year . . ."

Again I asked, "How long have you been praying about this?"

She continued, "My mom thinks I ought to go back to college, but my spouse says . . ."

This time, I squeezed her hand to get her attention. "How long have you been praying about this?"

Now with her undivided attention, Sheila answered me honestly, "Well, I haven't. I haven't prayed at all. I've talked things over with my colleagues, my mom, my spouse, and even my sisters — but I've left God out of the equation totally!"

How sad and how common! Remember to make God your first — not last — resource in any crisis.

> **Thought for the day:** Take Jesus' advice from verse 25 to heart: "And can any of you by worrying add a single hour to your span of life?" What am I worrying about that could be given to God in prayer?

40. Taking Refuge
by Tyler Connoley

Today's scripture: Psalm 18:1–3, 21–23, and 30–33

There was a time in my life when I left the Church and studied other religions. Though I chose to come back to Christianity, I still find much wisdom in Buddhist teachings, particularly those of Tich Nath Han, a Vietnamese Zen Buddhist monk now living in England.

Tich Nath Han teaches his followers to repeat the "three refuges" to themselves whenever they hear a bell, gong, or even a telephone ringer: *I take refuge in the Dharma. I take refuge in the Sangha. I take refuge in the Buddha.*

The Dharma is usually understood as the recorded teachings of the Buddha. Sangha means "group," and is any community of Buddhists. Buddha, for Tich Nath Han, means the "Buddha nature," which he believes we can all access.

I've taken this idea of the three refuges and adapted it to my own Christian practice, saying, *"I take refuge in the Word. I take refuge in the Church. I take refuge in the Christ."* I repeat the three refuges when I hear a church bell, gong, or sometimes a telephone.

Here's some of what I think as I say the three refuges to myself:

I take refuge in the Word: The Bible is a source of strength for me. I can go to God's Word for wisdom and comfort. I can also go there simply to hear how God has worked in the past, and will work in my future.

I take refuge in the Church: The Church has not always been a refuge for me, but I am so grateful for a community of believers who support me and challenge me. My Christian friends are also a refuge for me in times of testing.

I take refuge in the Christ: The same Spirit at work in Christ is at work in me. Jesus said, "I will ask the Father, and he will give you another Advocate, to be with you forever" (John 14:16). I can access the Holy Spirit at any time and in every situation. Or, as the Psalmist says, "my God, my rock in whom I take refuge" (Psalm 18:2).

Thought for the day: Next time you hear a bell, gong, or the telephone, say the three refuges to yourself and think about what they mean to you: *I take refuge in the Word. I take refuge in the Church. I take refuge in the Christ.*

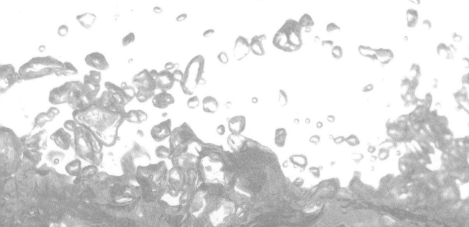

41. I Got You, Lord
by Steve Adams

Today's scripture: Galatians 5:22–23; 2 Peter 1:3–11

I believe that life is wonderful — but it takes a lot of patience, doesn't it?

It requires most of our energy to compete against sin and its consequences. Almost every day, there's something different to challenge us to the core. And when fellow Christians are the challenging element — when they say loving, committed same-sex relationships are wrong (or that "condoning" them is wrong, if you're an ally) — then even more patience is required. But, hey, no problem! Our God has an unlimited supply; all we need to do is tap into it!

The only way to deal with religious prejudice is to have lots and lots of fruit of the Spirit. Love helps us to shine God's light, even if some churches teach that LGBTQ people are immoral. Joy gives us the strength to endure Christians who believe it's their God-given duty to speak out against a vulnerable minority. Peace gives us the stability to maintain our presence of mind when fellow believers say same-sex couples weaken society.

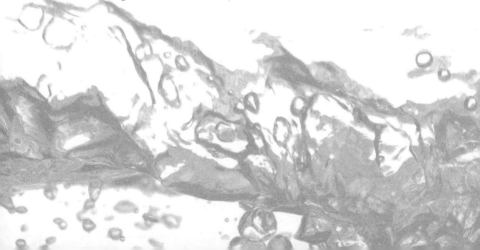

Patience enables us to go on — to never give up the fight. Kindness gives us the ability to gently explain a more thoughtful way of seeing God. Generosity motivates us to give our time to tell about a logical, yet faith-filled view of the Bible.

Faith gives us the vision to know that God will prevail in the end. Gentleness helps us use an easy hand with those who stubbornly adhere to their religious illogic. Self-control helps us continue looking to God as we deal with this doctrinal epidemic of ignorance.

Peter urges us to "make every effort" to support our faith with goodness, knowledge, self-control, endurance, godliness, mutual affection, and love. We can continue to live lives filled with the fruit of the spirit, and not be distracted by doctrines that could make us feel ashamed. Each of us can say, "I know, Lord, I've got you, and you've got me — forever!"

> **Thought for the day:** Thank you, Lord, for giving me the enthusiasm to assert the truth, knowing what a positive impact it will have on the souls of those who want to hear!

42. The Father's Gifts
by Theresa Benson

Today's scripture: Matthew 7:9–11

Having grown up in a low-income, single-parent home for most of my childhood, I had no experience buying "real" jewelry until just last year, when a department store was going out of business and I got some great 80-percent-off deals. Even then, my purchases were rather modest by most standards.

These days, I have a wonderful boyfriend who has often on the weekends taken me to the different jewelry stores here in the area to get a sense of my "jewelry style." One Saturday, he had me try on a diamond bracelet, which was beautiful and made me feel (I must admit) like a princess. I'd never had something so sparkly on my wrist before. He asked me to rate how much I liked it on a scale of 1 to 10.

After some deliberation, I rated it a conservative "8.9," even though in my heart it was like a 14.

Later that same weekend he took me to another store, and I saw a beautiful yellow- and white-gold bracelet that I just knew had to be much, much less expensive than the first bracelet, and so when he asked me how this one ranked, I immediately beamed that it was easily a 12 out of 10.

He gave me a puzzled look, and asked me if I was sure — was the modest bracelet really so much more beautiful to me, even though my face glowed when I had the other bracelet on?

He asked if we could talk about it, and I realized during the course of that conversation that I had been afraid to tell him what

I really liked. I was afraid for reasons having nothing to do with him — it was all old messages still running through my head from my childhood.

- If I tell him what I like, he might think that my tastes are too expensive or that I'm a snob and not like me anymore.

- If I tell him what I like, he might extend himself financially, and I would hate to impose on him like that for something so frivolous.

- If I tell him what I like, then he'll know exactly what to withhold in order to make me sad — he'll have some control over me, and I'll be vulnerable.

- If I tell him what I like, I just might get it, and then what would I do?

How amazing is that? The generous but simple act of my boy-friend wanting to know what kind of jewelry I like — he never even said he was going to *buy* anything — made all this old fear come up, and I was censoring myself before I even said a thing. If I do it with something this small, how many times have I done that with God?

We should be able to bring everything in our lives to God — the good and the bad — and ask for providence in all we do. But how many times have I felt that my dreams are too big or my problems too small to bother God with them? After all, God has much more important things to do. Besides, I'm probably asking for too much already.

I can't tell you how silly it looks now to write on paper that I'm afraid I might be asking the Infinite Creator for "too much."

Thought for the day: If a person I'm in relationship with can love me enough to ask my preferences in gift-giving, how much more does my Father in heaven want to know about me — my dreams and wishes, my desire for a clear purpose, and so much more!

43. *Why Worry?*
by Brent Walsh

Today's scripture: Matthew 6:25–34

The weathered evangelist takes a wrinkled handkerchief out of his back pocket and mops up beads of sweat from his brow. While he pauses, the congregation fills the silence with amens and hallelujahs. The humidity outside the open tent is dense, but inside it's suffocating. Moths and junebugs hover around the light bulbs that hang from tent supports. The preacher's voice is raspy as he brings his week-long revival to a close with this last sermon. All week he's been attacking things that bring good Christians down in their walk with God, and tonight he's got a new dragon to slay.

"Worry!" he bellows anew. "Worry is not just ill-advised, brothers and sisters! It's a sin against God!" His voice cracks as his finger stabs the air for emphasis. "It's your way of saying that you don't trust God! It's your way of taking your life out of God's hands! Don't do it, my friends! Don't let worry rob you of the happiness you deserve in the Lord!" Shouts erupt from all around. No one would dispute the good reverend! Isn't this what they've heard all their lives?

Have you ever been told that worry is a sin? Maybe you've just heard a compassionate soul say, "Don't worry — everything will work out." Or perhaps, "It won't do any good to worry; there's nothing you can do about it anyway." As well-intentioned (and sometimes true) as these statements might be, how often does a person hear these words and never think a thing about their troubles again?

Do you think there is ever a time when worry is good? Is it okay to worry about your children's safety when they don't arrive home at the usual time after school? Is it okay to worry when you hear an airplane crashed, and you don't know if it was the flight your spouse was on? Is it okay to worry about an aging mother when you realize she doesn't know who you are? Can we just take worry in general, put it all in a big box, and condemn it all?

We are told so often not to worry about money, because, after all, worrying about money isn't going to put it in your wallet, right? But if we don't worry at all about money, could we find ourselves without any? We are told not to worry about tomorrow, for tomorrow will take care of itself. But what if tomorrow is when your court date is scheduled to determine if you get custody of your children? We are told not to worry about our spousal relationship, but isn't a lack of concern over relationships the surest way to make them die? It's easy to parrot a phrase about how we must not worry, but how much thought is put into those statements?

Each of us will have to decide how much worry is warranted. Just as we cannot dismiss worry without a second look, let us also not dismiss the argument against worry that we find in today's scripture. I think Jesus gives us a generalization of a deeper truth.

Fire is useful to warm chilled bones, cook food, or purify metal — but it can't be allowed to spread uncontrolled. So it is, I believe, with worry. I think worry is natural and healthy in small doses. But if it is allowed to take over your life, it becomes destructive. I don't believe Jesus was addressing the worried mother waiting for a child at midnight. I do think, though, that Jesus knew how easily worry can become a habitual problem.

Maybe this is what the good preacher was talking about on that night inside the tent. Maybe he was talking about when worry replaces your trust in God, or when it replaces prayer. Don't let worry rob you of the happiness and fulfillment you deserve!

Thought for the day: God, help me to remember the lilies and to trust you.

44. *But I Don't Want to Go to Africa!*
by David Squire

Today's scripture: Isaiah 45:9–12

When I was a kid, maybe eight or ten, I somehow got the idea in my head that if I surrendered my will to God — if I really decided to follow Jesus whole-heartedly — that God would send me to Africa to be a missionary. And I thoroughly, sincerely, did not want to go to Africa.

A part of me really did want to do what God wanted me to do. But I thought that God would require me to do something I hated, something I'd have to endure, to show my devotion. It scared me to think about it, so I didn't. I just sort of coasted by, staying rather lukewarm in my commitment to follow Jesus.

Even the illustration in today's scripture — God as the potter, me as the clay — was a scary image then. If I wasn't a "perfect pot," God just might squish me on the celestial potter's wheel, or smash me to shards.

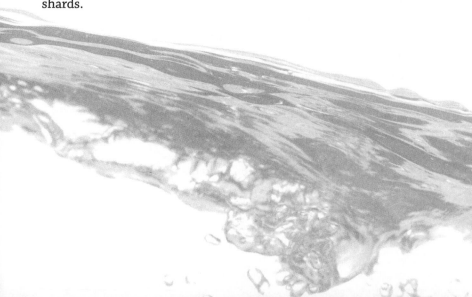

But I think we can see the potter/clay metaphor differently. Everything that's part of me — everything I love, everything I'm good at, every aptitude and ability, *everything that's in me already* — is part of the Sculptor's work. My lack of desire to go to Africa wasn't the clay rebelling against the Potter, but instead was part of how God has made this particular vessel. I wasn't *made* to be a missionary. But for someone else, that will be their source of joy.

I now believe that conforming to God's plan for me will bring me my greatest fulfillment. Only when I offer up what God has already fashioned and allow God's creative work to continue will I be all that I am destined to be.

Thought for the day: You're the potter, I'm the clay. God, continue your work in me — I can't wait to see what you're making!

45. Counting on God's Rule to Prevail
by Keith Phillips

Today's scripture: Habakkuk 3:17–19

I don't know that this passage of scripture is any more a favorite than many others; I just like to say the name of the prophet, *Habakkuk*.

Habakkuk happened to be proclaiming God's message when Nebuchadnezzar of Babylon was rising as the most powerful force in the Middle East, around 600 B.C.E. It's possible that an invasion of the Babylonians caused the agricultural devastation faced by God's people mentioned in verse 17 (the enemy's fault). It's equally possible that the land and the livestock had not prospered because God's people had broken God's covenant, either through laziness or by callous indifference (their fault). I'm not sure it really matters why bad things happen to God's people.

What does matter is our perspective and attitude right now. Bad things have happened; bad things are happening. Hopes are dashed, disappointment holds sway, the future looks bleak — or maybe not even quite that bad. Things just aren't going my way, and it hurts.

Hmmm . . . Could it be that, in my relationship with Jesus Christ, I'm paying more attention to me than to the relationship? I've heard

that happens in other significant relationships, to the detriment of the individual and the bond between the two. So when bad things happen, is it possible that I might need to reframe my thoughts and actions?

A favorite hymn begins, *"Turn your eyes upon Jesus; look full in his wonderful face; and the things of earth will grow strangely dim, in the light of his glory and grace."*

You know, not everything is going to go my way. And I suppose that's for the best. But I know Someone who has a greater vision than me and who is, in unseen ways, working the future out, including my own future. No matter how bad things are, the story is not over.

I'm in a relationship with Someone who loves me unconditionally, who has awesome power, and who frequently amazes me with wonderful gifts. Even when I don't like what's going on around me and in my life, I can rejoice, I can smile, I can sing!

> **Thought for the day:** How will my relationship with Jesus Christ adjust my perspective and attitude at the beginning of this day and throughout the day? Am I "counting on God's rule to prevail"?

46. *The Praise Test*
by Melody Merida

Today's scripture: Proverbs 27:21

My nephew, Connor, has become quite the swimmer. He is eleven years old and swims with a local swim club almost every day. They practice hours a day and have swim meets virtually every weekend competing against other clubs from around the United States. Frankly, I don't know how he does it. I get exhausted just watching him warm up for practice! He literally swims — and very well, I might add — for hours on end without much of a break.

Because I'm so enamored with his ability and because I admire such dedication to a sport, I tend to praise his efforts — a lot! When I first started heaping praises upon him a few years ago when he began swimming, it seemed like the right thing to do to build his confidence. I soon found out that my praises were having a negative effect on him. When I would say, "You were great in the 100-meter freestyle!" his response started to become, "I know, I beat everybody by a mile! Nobody on my team or the other teams came even close to me."

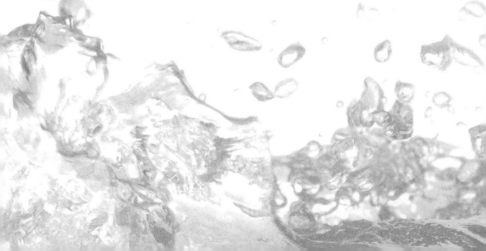

At first, I thought it was cute because he was so confident. Now it's been taken to an extreme. So my family and I are now much more careful with the type of praise we give to Connor. There is much more of an effort to build him up so that he feels good about himself but doesn't feel that he is superior to others.

Like my nephew, we are all tested when praise is heaped upon us. It's human nature — it's hard not to become full of ourselves when others are telling us how wonderful we are or what a wonderful job we've done. When praise comes our way, we have the opportunity to respond the way that Connor did, or to respond with humility, knowing that anything we achieve is a gift from God.

Thought for the day: When you are tested by praise (and you will be), how are you going to respond? Prepare now to acknowledge God when it happens so that you can respond humbly and pass the test!

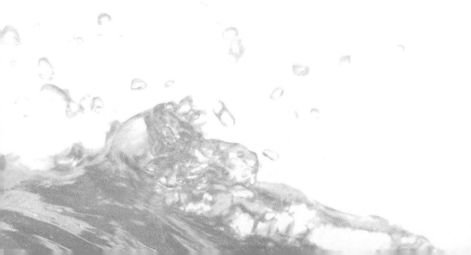

47. *One of the Family*
by David Squire

Today's scripture: Romans 8:15–17

About a year ago, my partner Dave and I adopted two dogs from rescue organizations. There's Chester, a beagle/border collie/something mix, who made himself at home almost from day one. Then there's Avery, the pit bull mix. Contrary to the breed's reputation, she's the sweetest dog you'll ever meet. And she was wary coming into our household — fearful, kind of nervous. We don't know much about Avery's life before we adopted her, but her fear leads us to believe that it wasn't very good.

When they were adopted, Chester and Avery hit the puppy jackpot. They've got everything they could ever need or want — good food and "cookies," rope toys and rawhide chews, a yard to chase rabbits in, and dads who provide pats and tummy rubs and don't mind (much) wiping their muddy paws.

Dave and I have both noticed that, in just the last couple of months, Avery has been wagging her tail more and is noticeably more at ease. It's taken her a while to let down her guard and feel "at home," but she's starting to understand that she's been adopted and

is safe here. Memories of cages and animal shelters and whatever came before are fading. She'll never have to go there again.

I see Christians who live as Avery was, and my heart grieves. We often live in such fear — fear that God is watching, waiting for us to slip up, so that we can be whipped and put in a cage for being "bad dogs." But we should be full of joy, because we live in God's presence — as *The Message Bible* puts it, we can say with adventurous expectation, "What's next, Papa?" (verse 15b). We "behave" not because we fear punishment, but because we don't want to interrupt the joy that comes from abiding close to the One who has adopted us.

We don't disown our dear puppies when they have muddy paws, and God doesn't toss us aside either. God will gently wipe away the dirt, all the while reassuring us that we're still part of the family. We've been adopted — we're here to stay.

Thought for the day: Does it feel "improper" to call God daddy? What am I afraid of?

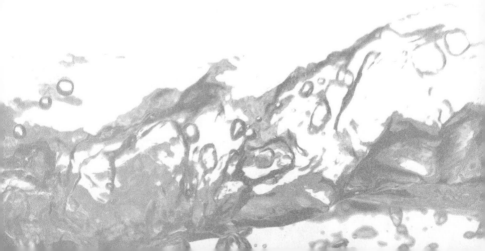

48. The Only Thing That Counts
by Tommy Chittenden

Today's scripture: Galatians 5: 2–6

You've probably seen those commercials showing students skipping from their classrooms at the conclusion of the last day of school, or employees running gleefully out the door of their workplace at the end of the day, signaling the arrival of a long-awaited vacation. It may only be a temporary hiatus for the students who must return in the fall or an even shorter time span for the vacationing employees, but what a wonderful feeling freedom brings to our minds and spirits — freedom from the authority of a teacher or from an employer's control over our time and activity.

While we often daydream about what that freedom will be like, basking in the thought of being able to do what we want, when we want — all it takes is the reality of that annoying alarm clock to summon us back to the obligations of school or work!

We should never let one day pass for which we don't thank our Creator that the freedom we know — through Jesus, as God's

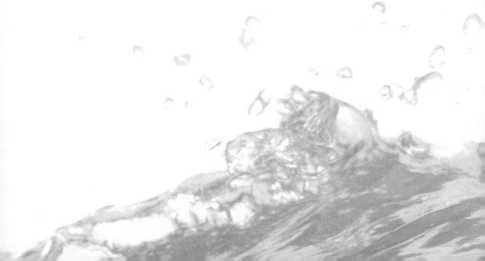

children — is not temporary. True liberty comes from realizing that Jesus is Lord! As his disciples, we are not bound to the dogma and obligations of institutionalized religion, but instead we are asked to believe the One who is revealed in the scriptures (John 5:39–40). Let's always measure our life by his standards, submit ourselves to his yoke, and exercise care to never place a yoke on others that is not of Jesus Christ. It can take us a long time to stop thinking that, unless everyone sees things as we do, they must be wrong. For most of us, we've been on the other end of this kind of treatment all too often.

There is only one true liberty — the liberty of Jesus at work in our conscience, enabling us to do what is right. Paul sums it up for us: "The only thing that counts is faith working through love" (verse 6b).

Thought for the day: Jesus said, "Go . . . and make disciples" (Matthew 28:19), not "Go . . . and convert them to your thoughts and opinions."

49. *Someone Understands Me!*
by Ben Lamb

Today's scripture: Romans 8:26–27

Have you ever had friends so close that they could finish your sentences and seem to read your mind? Whether or not you may think you have such a friend in the religious realm, the Bible assures us that we do: the Holy Spirit, whom Jesus sent after his ascension into heaven.

How many times have you seen "Heaven Speak 101" offered as a learning course? Me neither. The Holy Spirit could be thought of as the ultimate in translators — gathering up human thoughts and ideas, understanding them completely, and then delivering them instantly to our very Creator in the exact way that we wish we could. Personally, it's impossible for me to adequately express my feelings for God by using my own words.

I wish I'd read this verse as a child. I used to be self-conscious about praying. I thought that it had to be in front of people and aloud, and that I had to use a bunch of "thou," "hast," and "thine" type of words. Looking back, how insulting to God I was! The Creator of the universe surely understands the simple words that we speak silently and alone, too.

There have been moments in my life when my heart was so heavy with grief that I couldn't begin to convey it to God. Several years ago, my father was rapidly becoming so ill that it was beginning to seem he would die soon. I was sitting in a college classroom one evening.

When thinking of him, I felt like a caged, restless animal and wanted to be doing anything except listening to the professor's lecture. Suddenly, a sense of peace and calmness enveloped me. I knew that — no matter what happened — I would be able to endure the future. Dad coded unexpectedly directly in front of me, dying a few days later; but I'll always believe the Holy Spirit earlier conveyed my fears to God and instilled in me the reply, "I'll always be with you; be at peace about whatever lies ahead."

The Holy Spirit can convey our exuberant thoughts, too. Have you ever been listening to music, watching something, or hearing someone talking and were so moved by it that some tears filled your eyes, your emotions went on overload, and you couldn't think of anything to say? The Holy Spirit can work on our behalf during those times of happiness, too.

The next time your thoughts and feelings get stuck inside of yourself, remember the Holy Spirit is already interceding for you.

Thought for the day: Thank you, Jesus, for sending the Holy Spirit to be with us.

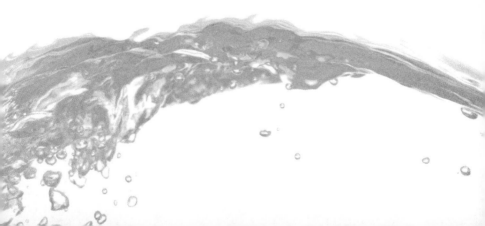

50. *Baby Steps*
by Tommy Chittenden

Today's scripture: Matthew 11:28–30

Kneeling and with outstretched arms, a father gently encourages his baby — about to become a toddler — with these words, "Come to me. You can do it, come to Daddy." I've anxiously watched my own sons (now young adults) let go of the object of their security and take those first few wobbly steps into my arms — truly one of those magical moments for any parent! The fear, insecurity, and doubt that new toddlers feel is soon gone when they consider the plea of Mom or Dad to unconditionally trust and are swept up with words of praise and confirmation.

At the most unexpected moments in our lives — moments of fear, failure, vulnerability, doubt, grief, and depression — there comes this gentle, encouraging whisper from Jesus: "Come to me." Personal contact with Jesus changes everything!

The attitude we must have in coming to him is that we have determined to let go of everything that has caused the exhaustion, listlessness, anxiety, and emotional torture that afflicts us. That determination causes us to "let go" — though we're wobbly at first — and commit all to him who extends his loving and welcoming arms.

"And I will give you rest" (verse 28b). I think Jesus is saying, "I

will sustain you, enable you to stand firm, show you how to walk when the burdens of life (our yoke) seem like too much." If we consider coming to Jesus as some kind of "get out of jail free" card we will undoubtedly be disappointed!

Instead his invitation, in reality, is a command — a call to discipleship by which we must single-mindedly and unresistingly let his yoke rest upon us. Only then can we expect to achieve liberty and enjoy true fellowship in the arms of Jesus. Only then can we find life's burdens and insecurities manageable by having access to God's power, which enables us to persevere in the right way! "His commands are not burdensome" (1 John 5:3b).

He is not necessarily saying, "I will put you to bed, hold your hand, and sing you to sleep." Rather he is saying, "I will get you out of bed — out of your listlessness and exhaustion, out of your condition of being half-dead while still alive — and I will penetrate you with the Spirit of Life so you can walk with the vitality and power that only the Son of God can give!"

Thought for the day: Jesus, please help me to be quiet and listen, so I can hear and respond as you invite me to "come . . . and receive your rest."

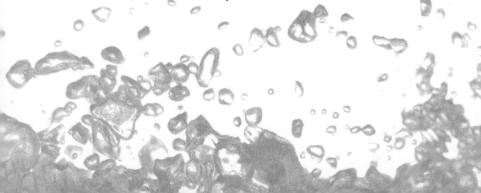

51. *Where Were You?*
by Jeff Miner

Today's scripture: Job 38:1–7 and 42:1–6

Whenever anything adverse happens in our lives, our first question is usually, "Why did God let this happen?" The question arises from our natural desire to want to understand. When we can't, we sometimes begin to question whether God cares — or even exists.

This is precisely where Job found himself. Job had experienced monumental tragedy: he lost all of his children in a natural disaster and then lost his own health. The book of Job records his quest to make sense of it all. Ultimately he can't, and his faith is in jeopardy.

That's when God steps in. After Job has asked all his questions — "Why? Why? Why?" — God's response, in essence, is, "You're too dumb to understand!" Granted, God's language is more diplomatic than that, but basically that's the point. For chapters on end, Job has been demanding to know why. Having listened to this endless questioning, it seems as if God is exasperated.

"Now I'm going to ask you some questions!" God says. What follows in chapters 38, 39, 40, and 41 is a long litany of questions about creation and reality. For example, God asks Job:

Where were you when I laid the foundation of the earth? Tell me if you have understanding. (38:4)

Have the gates of death been revealed to you, or have you seen the gates of deep darkness? (38:17)

Where is the way to the dwelling of light? (38:19)

Obviously, Job has no clue. No human — even the most brilliant — can comprehend the wonder of creation, the mystery of death, or the nature of light. To this day, scientists are forced to use inherently contradictory theories to explain the behavior of light.

When God ends this litany of questions, Job has gotten the point. Job says, "I have uttered what I did not understand, things too wonderful for me which I did not know" (42:3). Job finally understands that finite human beings can never hope to comprehend fully the nature of a reality designed by an Infinite Being.

In his own search for faith, a search that ultimately led him to Christ, mathematician Blaise Pascal reached the following conclusion: "There is nothing so consistent with reason as the denial of reason. For reason's last step is the recognition that there are an infinite number of things which are beyond it."

Really smart people understand how much they will never know. Although they still strive to understand as much as possible, they don't base their faith on their ability to rationalize every single act of God. God gives us enough "evidence" to reasonably believe, but there are many mysteries that we will not understand until we are elevated out of our limited human existence. As Paul said, "Now I know only in part. Then [in the next life] I will know fully" (1 Corinthians 13:12).

When I finally came to realize this in my own personal spiritual journey, I stopped "chasing my tail" and was freed from the impossible task of understanding everything. I still have lots of questions. I still take logic as far as it will carry me. But when I've gone as far as I can and yet fall short of understanding, my faith is not at risk.

Thought for the day: It only makes sense that a cosmos designed by an Infinite Being will be perplexing to a finite being. Stop chasing your tail!

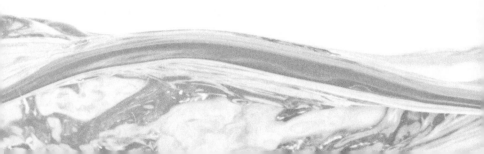

52. *Hey God, Wanna Come to a Party?*
by Theresa Benson

Today's scripture: Matthew 6:34

There it was, almost 5:00 p.m., and I had 15 guests invited to a get-together at my house at 6:00. Scrambling to put the finishing touches on a quilt I'd promised to make for a friend's granddaughter, I hadn't started putting the food out. I hadn't walked the dog or showered yet, and everything for the mulled wine I'd planned to make, which takes a couple hours to simmer to start to taste really good, was still in the grocery bags from my run to the store that morning. And I still had a couple presents to wrap and needed to pack for a trip for which I was leaving bright and early the next morning.

Who planned this party, anyway? I certainly had all the ingredients for full-blown panic to set in, culminating in a mad rush around the house trying to get everything together before the doorbell rang. But, still recovering from reconstructive foot surgery, my "mad dash" was still like a turtle on valium.

I needed some major help here. I had recently taken the basic discipleship classes at our church, and one of the things we discussed and practiced was really cultivating a relationship with God — talking to God, asking for help, thanking God for all the blessings we receive every day.

For me, this has historically been a scary proposition, as my image of God had been damaged by my relationships with adults as a child, and I thought of God as angry, withholding, and punishing. I am working to improve my image of God, but unlearning something 34 years in the making can be a tough job.

However, putting trust in the things I'd learned, and in the examples that my friends at our church have shared with me about a God who loves me and is intimately interested in creating an abundant life with me, I realized that, if I'm going to be in relationship with someone, I certainly better not leave that One off the guest list to my party!

Right there, in that moment, I decided to stop panicking and talked with God, and gave a last-minute invitation:

God, I'm frantic about getting everything done in time for my party. I'm sorry I didn't think to invite you sooner, but I need your help. You are infinite, and in the grand scheme of things, time means nothing to you. I need a miracle here — can you stretch out time or something so I can get done everything I need to and send your Holy Spirit and help me be calm when my guests arrive? Please be with us tonight at this get-together; bless everyone who will be here and those who couldn't make it. Thank you for keeping everyone safe tonight and for helping make this a lot of fun. Love you!

Shortly after this, I got a phone call that a couple folks were going to be late, and would arrive around 6:30. A couple more called to say they, too, would be delayed. Amazingly, I had my shower taken, the dog walked, the food out, the music going by five after six, and still had a few minutes to sit with Abby the Wonder Poodle and enjoy the warmth of my home before my guests arrived.

Thought for the day: Whenever I'm stressed, I'll ask myself: "Did I invite God to this party?"

53. *My Tattoo*
by Julie Walsh

Today's scripture: John 7:1–24

It is cited on my license plate. It is the root of my e-mail address. It is prominent in my online profile. It even appeared in a fortune cookie I opened from a Chinese restaurant years ago. It's my little life mantra from John 7:24 — *"Do not judge by appearances, but judge with right judgment."* An ironic quotation for a woman with pink and purple hair, right? For the record, I chose this passage in high school when I was sporting my "natural" hair color — a confession I will not disclose in this forum.

John 7:24 also sounds a little preachy, doesn't it? How do I get off telling the world what they need to do? Sure, it's nice to see people from my rear-view mirror pointing at my license plate. I've become a good lip-reader, able to distinguish common remarks like, "It must be from the Bible." And, of course, I hope that they will gain a little insight of their own when they flip open the pages of scripture. Honestly, though, this passage serves as a reminder for me more than for anyone else. I need to hear it over and over, so I've tattooed it on my heart.

The story in John 7 begins by explaining how Jesus intentionally avoids creating a public display in Judea. However, out of respect for the Jewish Feast of the Tabernacles (the harvest festival memorializing the redemption of Israel from slavery), Jesus follows behind in

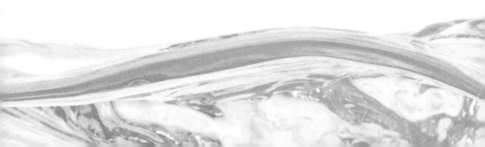

private. Midway through the festival, Jesus begins teaching; when questioned about his authority, Jesus claims to be not just another rabbi, but a prophet whose teaching comes from God. Jesus then spells out the alternative in verse 18: "Those who speak on their own seek their own glory."

Jesus then addresses his opponents who misunderstand the commandment about keeping the law on the Sabbath. Jesus explains that saving lives and expressing God's spirit of love and mercy by doing good should take precedence over the letter of the law. He then concludes that the way we see the world should be through God's eyes and not our own. Righteous judgment means that we seek God's will and God's truth in everything, putting our own prejudices and preconceptions aside.

It is easy for me to think that I can quickly sum a person up by an external appearance, by an off-the-cuff remark, or even by more regular encounters that lead me deeper into a person's personality. John 7:24 reminds me that I must not judge by any outward or superficial judgments, but by God's worth and by the gifts and graces of God's Spirit in them. I also apply John 7:24 to the circumstances of daily life by sacrificing my own desired outcomes, and seeking and trusting instead in God's will.

Thought for the day: I will focus on seeing the people around me through God's eyes, and not through my own.

54. *Only You Can Be You*
by Tyler Connoley

Today's scripture: Daniel 1:3–7

In these verses, the author tells us Daniel and his friends were handed over to Ashpenaz, a character who will become important as Daniel's story unfolds. Unfortunately, however, most English translators obscure one of the important aspects of Ashpenaz's story. The New Revised Standard Version calls him the "palace master" and The Message Bible calls him "the head of the palace staff." A more literal translation would be Chief Eunuch (Hebrew, *Sar HaSarisim*).

The ancient Babylonians had a common practice of taking the best and the brightest young men from conquered nations and bringing them home to be officials in the king's cabinet. The idea was that these men would be able to advise the king and help him assimilate the conquered peoples. However, because the Babylonians didn't want these foreigners intermarrying with Babylonian women, they would first castrate them before they allowed them to hold high government positions. In Hebrew, these men are called *sarisim*, which means "eunuchs," but many translators prefer to call them by their job description — officials or palace staff — perhaps to protect squeamish readers.

Why does this matter? Well, the fact that Ashpenaz was the Chief Eunuch tells us something about the men who were placed under his care — they were probably eunuchs as well. That means Daniel,

one of the great heroes of the Bible, was almost certainly a castrated man.

For those of us who are lesbian, gay, bisexual, or transgender, this is significant. It means Daniel was also sexually different. Like us, he might have been thought of by his colleagues in the palace as "not a real man." Like us, he would have been unable to have a "normal" relationship with the opposite sex. And, like us, he may have had days when he wondered why God let this happen to him.

However, Daniel also allowed God to use him where he was and as he was. Daniel didn't just accept his lot; he excelled by God's grace. There were avenues available to him as one of the eunuch officials that would not have been available otherwise, and he used those to great advantage. If he had remained a bright young man and married a bright young woman in Israel, we might never have heard of him. But, because he became a eunuch in the palace in Babylon and allowed God to use him in that role, he became one of the great heroes of the Bible.

> **Thought for the day:** What avenues are open to you because of the things that have happened to you in the past? Are you willing to let God use you where you are and as you are?

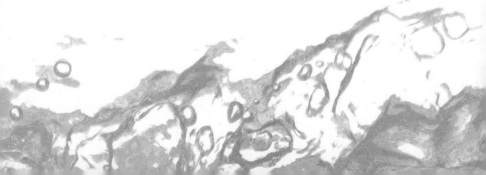

55. *Room, Even for Me!*
by Mark Shoup

Today's scripture: John 14:1–3

Back when I was in my early 20s, I was a mess! It's a common story in our congregation (and elsewhere): I knew not only that I was gay and couldn't change that, but also that God was real. This would have been no problem except that my fundamentalist upbringing said that gays could not be Christians in good standing, and would not get to heaven if they didn't change. There was great conflict in me as these two undeniable forces tried to exist simultaneously in my head and soul.

All I could see to do was run away from the conflict, and I ended up being a reluctant and closeted gay man, and a distant and skeptical Christian.

Even in the midst of all this conflict, there were still a couple of verses in the Bible that gave me comfort. This passage from John was one of them. Reading it at that time in my life, it seemed to be saying that maybe, even against what my church was saying, there might be a place for me in heaven. That maybe one of those dwelling places could even be for people like me who found themselves unable

to stop being gay, but still believed. It was this sort of "call from the Governor" theology that probably kept me from doing something irreversible at a time when I didn't think my life was worth very much.

Now, of course, I know a lot more about the Bible and how some have twisted its meaning around at the expense of folks like me. I know that there are a lot more places in the Bible where it says that people like me are loved by God, and will inherit the Kingdom of Heaven.

But it still comforts me to know that the Kingdom isn't just for a narrow segment of the population — God has space for lots of different people. Besides, it might get pretty boring if we all had to be like Pat Robertson or Oral Roberts.

There is even a place for people like me!

Thought for the day: God, thank you for the wideness of your mercy! Help me to always keep in mind: Am I making space in my life for all kinds of people, like you do, or am I keeping some people out?

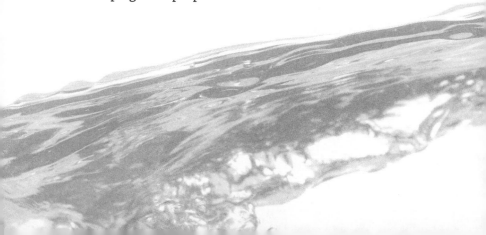

56. *Why So Downcast?*
by Tyler Connoley

Today's scripture: Psalm 42

I was having one of those mornings when God felt very distant. To be honest, I was feeling agnostic leaning toward atheistic. My soul felt dark and empty, and I thought, "I must be the worst Christian on the planet — no one could be more faithless than I am today."

However, I decided to read the psalm for that morning anyway. I've been taught that when you're thrown into the deep end of the lake, you should just pretend like you can swim. Tread water until you reach dry land or someone comes to rescue you. This particular morning, I was sure no one would come to rescue me, because no one was out there.

So I prayed, "God please make yourself real to me. I can't feel you this morning."

And I opened my Bible to the psalm: "As a deer longs for flowing streams, so my soul longs for you, O God" (verse 1).

"Well," I thought, "this Psalmist certainly felt better about God than I do today. He loved God and longed for God, and I'm not even sure God exists."

Then I read on: "My soul thirsts for God, for the living God. When shall I come and behold the face of God?" (verse 2).

Suddenly, I realized that this Psalmist knew exactly how I felt. Like me, he was longing for a glimpse of God's face, for some proof that God was not dead but alive.

The psalm continues: "My tears have been my food day and night, while people say to me continually, 'Where is your God?'"

And the Psalmist then recalls how he used to lead processions, and to sing and shout with thanksgiving to God. He has hope that he will feel that way again, but he insists that he doesn't feel God's presence today.

I have to admit, like the Psalmist, I didn't suddenly sense God's presence and know that everything was going to be fine. However, as I read this psalm, I felt less alone. I knew I was not the only one to have days when God felt distant. And, with the Psalmist, I was able to say: "Why are you cast down, O my soul, and why are you disquieted within me? Hope in God; for I shall again praise [God], my help and my God" (verse 5).

Thought for the day: Do you have days when you can't feel God's presence, and wonder if God even exists? You're not alone. Together, we can hope in God, for we shall again praise God.

57. Enjoy the Journey!
by Theresa Benson

Today's scripture: Ecclesiastes 6:6–9

I was listening to the *Oprah & Friends* program the other day on my way to Michigan, and they had a guy on who has a doctorate in "Happiness" — who knew?! Anyway, he was talking about a concept called "destination addiction." Wow, did that sound familiar!

Oprah's makeup artist came on then, and talked about how, for years and years, he wanted a house of his own, really wanted that house. He imagined the parties he and his partner would have there, and how happy they would be.

People would tell him, "Oh, you have a lovely apartment. If you get a house, you'll want to fill it up with furniture. And you'll have all the obligations that come with a house." But he insisted, "No, I'm OK with the furniture I have. I just want a house, a lovely little house."

Finally, he got that house, and what's the first thing that crept into his head? Oh, this house isn't put together quite right. I need some new furniture for this wonderful new house! Once he had the furniture, and everything "just so," his partner of several years, stressed out by the burdens and obligations of being a homeowner, chose to leave the relationship — and here was Oprah's makeup artist, with the house he'd always wanted and the furniture he thought would be beautiful in that home, all ready to have that party. But he was sadly alone, lonely, and just wishing for his apartment, his old furniture, and his old life.

Why do I tell this story? Does this mean we should just give up altogether and accept the status quo? Heck no! Goals are good things to have. Can you imagine the Israelites still in slavery just saying, "Well, that's that, no use in thinking there's something better out there"? But it does mean that we should be grateful for that "bird in the hand" and realize the blessings we have all around us today. Getting that new house won't make us happier. Getting a new job or a promotion, or new furniture, won't make everything better.

Letting myself become addicted to the next thing and the next, each time lying myself into believing that then everything will be better, is just that — lying. The only thing that can make me happier is God — and, with God's help, me.

Even the Israelites, in their time in the narrow places, still loved each other and loved God and did what they could to make what they had the best they could make it, all the while believing in a goal greater than themselves.

So I'm going to be grateful for the bird in my hand today — and bring God into the planning and goal setting for the next steps in my life, that I may move from being addicted to the next destination, and enjoy the journey God has set out for me.

Thought for the day: Can I be grateful for what I have and where I am — or am I "destination addicted"?

58. *The Gods Have Come Down to Us!*
by Deb Doty

Today's scripture: Acts 4:36–37, 14:8–18

One of my favorite Bible people is Barnabas — the "son of encouragement." But the passage in Acts 14 is not one of the better-known ones concerning Barnabas and his protégé, Paul. That's probably because it's sorta weird — Paul and Barnabas end up being mistaken for Greek gods after a crippled man gets healed.

Picture Barnabas frantically trying to dissuade the crowd from offering sacrifices to Paul and him as the supposed ruler of the gods and his son, the messenger! Maybe he thinks, "What have I gotten myself into? All we did was encourage a man with God's healing — and now look! Better talk fast before we're up to our armpits in dead oxen!"

So he and Paul try to re-direct the people to the real source of encouragement: God. They tell the crowd that it is the living God who gives them "rains from heaven and fruitful seasons," filling them with food and their hearts with joy. And yet the people cry out, "The gods have come down to us in human form!" as they toss garlands. It takes quite a bit of talking from Barnabas and Paul to finally get them calmed down.

Now we can say, "How silly those people were, mistaking Barnabas and Paul for gods!" But were they completely silly? In their culture, the gods visited mortals often. They all knew lots of stories about such visits. So they were totally prepared to welcome the divine. And in this preparedness, they put us to shame.

How often do we fail to recognize God's encouragement when our stomachs are filled with food and our hearts with joy? How many times have we thought God is too far away and too busy to care about us? Yet God has and does walk among us. As Paul repeatedly preached, God walked among us in Jesus. And God walks among us today through the presence of the Holy Spirit.

Maybe the folks in Lystra weren't so goofy after all.

Thought for the day: Let's be prepared to see God today.

59. *To Be Like God*
by Robert Ferguson

Today's scripture: Luke 6:36

My grandmother used to tell me to be careful how I treat others, because you never know whose arms you may fall into one day. I have tried to live by this little adage, but I must admit, it continues to be a challenge.

When I first started to meditate on this passage, my mind immediately went to co-workers who challenge my attempts to show mercy. Whether it's the 7:00 a.m. bright-eyed lady who is ready to go first thing in the morning, or the guy who has to ask a thousand more questions during an organizational meeting that has already passed the three-hour mark, I am challenged at work to show mercy as God has shown mercy to me.

Recently I have had a slew of car maintenance issues. If you have ever had to deal with car dealership mechanics over expensive car repairs, I am sure you will agree with me that it is difficult to show mercy when presented with a repair bill that rivals the national debt. I must admit my attitude was far from merciful and Christian as I reluctantly laid my credit card down on the service desk.

Every day we have opportunities to show mercy as God has shown mercy to us. Some situations are just uncomfortable and

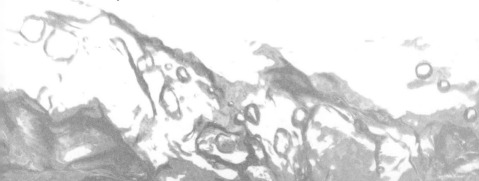

challenging to our own will. Others are challenging because the recipient may not, as we see it, deserve our mercy. Someone who offends us, disrespects us, or — say it isn't so — trespasses against us may deserve to feel a little bit of our anger or displeasure.

It is during these times when we are called to model and reflect the love, grace, and mercy that God has shown each of us. In our reading today we learn that it is not of God to constantly focus on what others have done or are doing to us. It is much better to focus on what God has done for every one of us. When we forget the many mercies and blessings we receive, brand new each day, it is reflected in how we treat others and how we respond to others.

Let us remember that we do not deserve God's mercy. We never could do anything that would prove us worthy of the love of God. Except for the soul-saving sacrifice of Jesus Christ, we would all be eternally separated from God and unable to receive forgiveness or grace.

So we thank God today for showing mercy to us — and we'll show that gratitude by the way we show mercy to those we come in contact with everyday. In some very small way, we can be like God!

Thought for the day: God, with everyone I encounter today, help me to show mercy. Help me to be like you!

60. *Unclaimed Blessings*
by Theresa Benson

Today's scripture: 1 Kings 1

Sometimes I really need to be reminded not to be so hard on myself and to remember just how far I've come. I recently had a conversation with my neighbor, Lynn, that made that point really clear.

I'm off work again for my second surgery, and my neighbors have been incredible about helping me with Abby the Wonder Poodle while I'm unable to get around. Lynn comes over in the morning to take her for a walk.

Usually, we'll get in a conversation about current events, or about how my foot is doing, or how remarkable all my friends have been in helping out around my house. But occasionally, as this morning, we'll go deep, and I was telling Lynn how I'd gotten in to Duke, Purdue, and Northwestern, and had passed the first round of application stuff at MIT, before my Mom announced, "Theresa, you can go anywhere you want as long as it's Iowa State University."

Now, I've told that story a zillion times, and every time someone asks me why I decided to get my electrical engineering degree, and I'm so hardened to it by now that I don't realize just how sad the story can sound. But this morning, it struck a nerve in Lynn, and she started tearing up and telling me just how unfair a decision that was, and that if I was her daughter, she'd have a "Wheel of Fortune" party where my friends, family, and I could spin the wheel to see what school I might end up at. What a blessing, she thought, and how terrible I wasn't able to receive it.

And with that conversation, I got the "permission" I needed to get angry about it for myself, to get frustrated about feeling stuck, and to feel compassion for the scared high school senior who was so afraid of her Mom that she didn't stand up for her future.

I am absolutely wowed by Bathsheba's willingness to stand up for her son Solomon with King David. Can you imagine? All those preparations had been made, the King was ill and dying, and she and her son had been slighted for the coronation. If the Theresa who made the decision to go to Iowa State were Bathsheba, she probably would have turned inward and thought that perhaps King David had changed his mind, that he no longer felt her son Solomon was "enough" to ascend the throne, or that she'd done something wrong — and, without warning, Adonijah was being crowned king instead.

And she would have lived under Adonijah's rule, feeling trapped, frustrated, sad, and out of place, all because she didn't speak up for herself and her son.

I had my "Nathans" in high school — teachers who thought highly of me and encouraged me to go to the school of my dreams and study whatever I felt I'd succeed in. But instead of listening to their wise counsel, and going to my Mom and saying, "Haven't you taught me all my life to be myself and to do what's best for me? Shouldn't I go to one of these other schools instead of Iowa State, since I have the aptitude, scholarships, and opportunity?" I shied away, and while I have had a good life (as I'm sure Bathsheba and Solomon might have had), for so long I've felt empty inside, mourning the missed opportunities and questioning if I'm fulfilling my purpose.

Thought for the day: It's my hope today that we might all speak up for ourselves; and for parents to speak up for your children — that we might all surely know that we're walking the path God has planned for us and truly receiving the blessings God gives us.

61. *Upon a Rock and a Hard Place*
by Ben Lamb

Today's scripture: Psalm 62

Everybody on planet earth knows what a rock is. What a brilliant way to describe God.

Huh? How can something so simple — and at a glance, mundane — possibly describe the creator of the universe?

God is compared to a mighty and strong impenetrable boulder that serves as the foundation of our faith, and also for the safe haven in which we may perpetually be hidden.

"Yeah, okay," I hear you saying, "that's all well and good for preachin' from the keyboard, Ben, but what about the toils of everyday life that slap me around? What am I supposed to do when all you-know-what breaks loose?" I admit I've shouted that same painful cry into my own mirror at times.

But verse 5 sheds some encouraging light: "For God alone my soul waits in silence, for my hope is from [God]." Even when all else may seem to be in the worst possible condition, my soul is still being cared for by God. And that's really the most important component of my entire being, because my soul is what remains after the rest of me is kaput.

Most of the time, however, we aren't in the deepest of deep despair. It's comforting to remember that God wants us to pour out our hearts at any time to this fortress that shall never be shaken.

God is always a refuge for us that is infinitely more reliable than any human. The Psalmist states that if you could put God and any human on balances (scales), the worth of the human would be so insignificant in comparison that their side would "go up." Yet, later on in the Bible, we find out about God's plan of salvation that involves Jesus and the horrific price they both paid purely for humanity's sake; kind of blows one's mind, doesn't it?

Life is filled with some shaky episodes. Thank God — literally — for God being a solid rock upon which we can always rely for a strong footing.

Thought for the day: "Rock climbing" with God is a great experience. No expensive equipment necessary; just an open heart.

62. *Steadfast*
by Tyler Connoley

Today's scripture: Psalm 118:26–29

The Hebrew word at the end of this text, *hesed,* is translated "steadfast love" in the New Revised Standard Version and "love" in *The Message Bible,* but it actually means something more like loyalty or fidelity. This word represents the relationship of someone who has the power to help you or not, and who then chooses to help. It could also refer to someone who has the choice to leave you or not, and who then chooses to stay. In her book on *hesed,* Katherine Doob Sakenfeld calls it "faithfulness in action."

One of my friends recently rescued a pit bull. Max, the dog, was abused by breeders who used him as "bait" to teach other dogs to fight. Those breeders perpetrated the worst kind of disloyalty and infidelity on this beautiful animal, and he is understandably skittish of new acquaintances. However, in just the few short weeks that he's lived with my friend, Max has begun to relax. With consistent kindness and loyalty, Max's new family believes they'll be able to help him recover from the trauma of his past.

This is how God works with us. We may have experienced people who treated us wickedly in the past, but God practices active faithfulness with us. God is patient, loyal, kind, steadfastly loving, and willing to spend however long it takes to win back our confidence. All of these actions of God are encompassed in the phrase, "God's *hesed* endures forever."

This is also one of the ways we can be the face of God to one another. Verse 26 says, "Blessed is the one who comes in the name of the Lord." When we practice "faithfulness in action," we are fulfilling that mandate. As I said, verse 29 refers to the fact that God has the power to stay or go, the power to help or not, and then God chooses to stay and help. By emulating God's *hesed*, and practicing this kind of loyalty with our friends and loved ones, we bless those we are staying with and helping, but we also find ourselves blessed in return. That's the promise of verse 26.

> **Thought for the day:** Have you had someone abandon you in the past? Rest in the fact that God will never abandon you. Is there someone who needs your loyalty? Be the face of God to that person today.

63. *Just Keep Singing*
by Keith Phillips

Today's scripture: 1 John 4:16–19

Why do I worry so much? Why am I too often afraid?

My guess is that, in part, it's a fear of the unknown combined with a known dynamic of cause and effect. As one into whom western linear logic has been ingrained, I am easily convinced that the bad stuff that happens to me is a result of previous bad choices and bad actions. The corollary to this is that, because I know myself to be imperfect, frequently feeling like a misfit by this world's standards, facing the potential consequences of what I do is not a pretty picture.

But then there is the grace of God. For some reason, and I really can't tell you why, God seems to love me. I assure you it has nothing at all to do with what I have done or not done, with having followed the rules. It seems that God simply loves me, just as I am.

And this is the Creator and Sustainer of the cosmos who loves me! God is not bound by western linear logic. God is above that, and

God demonstrates that regularly in my life with serendipitous surprises every day. God's grace forgives me, restores me, and empowers me. I am a living example that good things, wonderful things, blessed things, transforming things happen to bad people, imperfect people, people who are misfits.

Remembering that is the trick, though, because I'm surrounded with voices and experiences that scream at me that I am not good enough, that I haven't followed the rules, that I fail, that I don't deserve to be loved. All day long I must refocus on God and on God's perfect love which casts out fear.

Evening is fast becoming one of my favorite movies. Vanessa Redgrave stars as a mother who from her death bed reviews her long life. She worked in New York clubs, singing for "drunks and tourists," but at the end she looks back and says, "There are no mistakes; just keep singing."

Thought for the day: I know God loves me. How will I see God's hand at work today, transforming my "mistakes," as I keep singing?

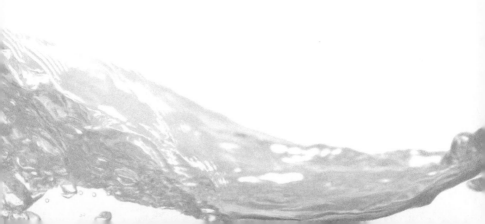

64. *Victory*
by Robert Ferguson

Today's scripture: 1 Corinthians 10:1–13

Temptation is a reality that has haunted every generation since Adam and Eve. However, we don't have to give in to temptation or get caught up in sin. We do have victory.

I know it sounds good on paper, but living it seems to be a daily challenge full of pitfalls and snares. As we look at 1 Corinthians, we find some meaningful answers. First, we can learn from others' mistakes. Second, we must believe that God's power is always available to us. Finally, we must abstain as best we can from evil. Following these three simple lessons reminds us that we have victory.

We learn from the mistakes made by others. Like warning signs, they show us the danger in going the wrong way. Here Paul shows us how the Jews were tempted, how they yielded, and how they paid the price for doing so. We have victory by learning not to repeat their mistakes.

Because of God's divine power, we are able to win over evil and temptation. If we take our challenges and shortcomings to God in prayer and listen for guidance and instruction, we can overcome all things. Our spiritual ancestors provoked God during their desert experience by doubting God's power to provide for them. They gave in to a lack of trust in God and began to complain and worry. Paul warns the Corinthians not to succumb to similar faults.

As in Corinth, our society today seems plagued with violence and a lack of love and respect for one another. Human suffering seems to be out of control — the fruit of greed, lack of compassion, and selfishness. When we strive to have a Christ-like mind and stay God-focused, we can avoid many of the sins that befall humanity. Turn away from those things that separate us from the will of God, a healthy lifestyle, and compassion for our brothers and sisters.

Thought for the day: Trust God and know that victory is ours. This Christian life must always strive to be a beacon of light in an otherwise dark world. Be encouraged to brighten your corner of the world today.

65. I Will Never Leave You, or Forsake You by Christen Peters

Today's scripture: 2 Corinthians 4:8–9

Anybody who thinks God lacks a sense of humor has not met the same God that has been with me lately.

When I was asked to write on these verses, I chuckled at how my perception of them is so different today than it would have been three months ago. At that time, I'd have thought that it would be easy. "God's always with you, tribulation makes the trip worthwhile, footprints in the sand — yada, yada, yada." God had other plans for me. God's plan was to give me some measure of the experience myself.

It is unlikely that I will ever know persecution like that of the early Christians. It's unlikely that I will ever be arrested and stoned to death for professing my faith in Jesus Christ. It's unlikely that I will ever have to guard my movements, relying on others to provide for my every need as I try to make safe passage to the next town.

It is almost guaranteed, though, that the time will come again when I will grieve the loss of a loved one, or grieve that a loved one is facing seemingly insurmountable troubles, or watch as good friends painfully dissolve their relationship and wonder if I'm doing all I can to make sure my relationship with my spouse doesn't meet the same end.

There were days when I wanted so badly to feel God's presence — but was too focused on what was going on without to pay attention to what was going on within.

One night as hot tears flowed, I found Joshua 1:5 — "I will not fail you, or forsake you" — running through my mind. In response to the thought I started humming *"Oh God, you are my God. And I will ever praise you."*

Something about my relationship with God happened in that moment. I think I finally absorbed that God really is always with me and will never leave me or forsake me. Since that moment, each obstacle I encounter seems to be accompanied by a song of praise that pushes its way past my instinct to grumble.

The only exception to that was when the reverse osmosis water filtration system blew up last night — no song of praise this time, but I could swear I heard God chuckling with me.

> **Thought for the day:** I don't think God leaves me in times of trouble — but my focus sometimes leaves God in times of trouble. Help me, dear Lord, to always keep you first in my thoughts.

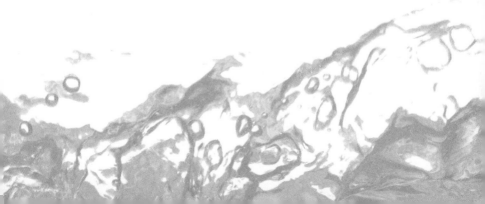

66. *To Whom It Is Given*
by John Seksay

Today's scripture: Matthew 19:11–12

I recently found an early attempt to start a journal when I was first coming out. It was March 1993 and had only one entry. It reads:

I'm not sure how to lay to rest the years of painful silence that surround my inner child — the sense of abandonment and betrayal by everything he believed in. Such is puberty for the gay child/teen. What balm exists for the loss of self-esteem and the absolute absence of any positive self-image?

God has shown me how the Word addresses this very issue.

Today's scripture passage first came to my attention when I started attending our church and read *The Children Are Free*. What an overwhelming sense of acceptance and reconnection to God began with these events! Unlike my upbringing in the Roman Catholic Church, God didn't see me as evil, corrupt, or "intrinsically disordered." Jesus had known, and spiritually accepted with great compassion, men like me. He acknowledged my existence without contempt or judgment!

But read carefully everything that is said in the scripture. Jesus opens the topic by saying, "Not everyone can accept this teaching, but only those to whom it is given" (verse 11). He finishes with the statement, "Let anyone accept this who can" (verse 12b).

This calls up another painful memory from my struggles as an adult. When I first brought up this issue as an adult with my parents,

I was married with kids. Mom was the coach and mentor most often sought out by all the kids. She didn't reject me outright, but steered me toward counseling, where I was given a multiple question test. I will never forget the look in her eyes when the results of the test indicated that I "officially wasn't gay." I knew then that my mother's deepest love was reserved for a son she didn't really have, but desperately wanted. I never let her see the gulf that event opened in my heart.

After finally coming out, I did experience acceptance from my siblings and children, and I came to understand what Jesus was saying. Only the people willing to love me unconditionally could see me as I truly am; those who brought other expectations in their hearts would remain fixed on their own internal image of me. It is the same with Jesus' teachings — often our internalized prejudices about what is right or good literally close our hearts to his words.

Eunuchs were also a very difficult subject for Jews to address, because the cultural roles for male and female, parent and child, were deeply ingrained, as they remain in many societies today. Was it just circumstance that led Philip, an apostle of Christ from a Hellenistic background, to meet with the eunuch from Ethiopia on the wilderness road? I like to believe that God knows the limits of God's servants, as well as their abilities, when God calls them to a task.

Jesus recognizes the challenge by warning us that not everyone will have the spiritual capacity to accept us as we are. One of our major challenges as Christians is to love ourselves as we are, and still have compassion for those who lack the spiritual capacity to do likewise.

Thought for the day: My prayer for today is that my love for Jesus and his teachings will also be unconditional. May I see and hear every blessing they have to offer!

67. *Seeking Perfection*
by David Zier

Today's scripture: 2 Corinthians 12:5–10

There was a time in my life where I was plagued by disappointment. If I got an A, but did not score 100, I was disappointed. If I messed up one note in my clarinet solo during the spring concert, I was heartbroken. If I won the match at tennis even though I lost a set, I felt like a loser. No one ever got on my case or made me feel this way — I was my own worst enemy.

As far as God was concerned, I felt the same way. No matter how good I tried to be, or what I would do in the name of Christ, it always seemed that I was never doing anything good enough or important enough to really matter. I never thought I was going to end up in hell, but I sure did a great job of putting myself there on my own. I was reluctant to ever try to do anything for God for fear that it would never be good enough.

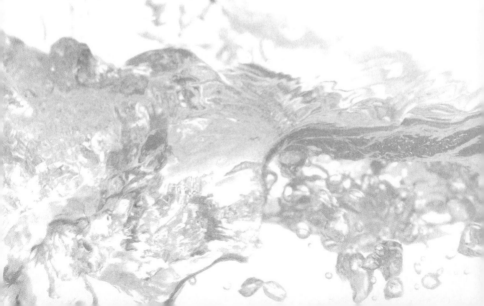

In today's passage, Paul is telling us that we don't have to be perfect. Paul tells us that God's grace is sufficient for us to overcome our feelings of insufficiency. In fact, Paul suggests that God's power shines more brightly when we are weak. We are to be content with who we are and allow the power of Christ to dwell within us.

Over the years I have pondered why I put myself through so much turmoil. I realize that all God asks of me is to do my best. The rest is up to God.

> **Thought for the day:** Instead of thinking about your imperfections and shortcomings, think about how God's power can work through your weakness.

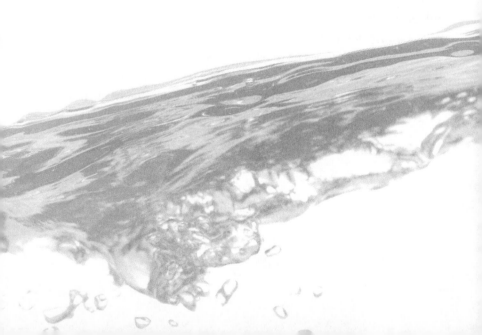

68. Y-E-E-E-U-U-URRR SAFE!
by Steve Adams

Today's scripture: Colossians 3:15; Hebrews 7:25

It was my turn at bat, the time I dreaded most in Little League softball games. The umpire called three strikes and then bellowed in that big voice of his, "Y-e-e-e-u-u-r-r-r OUT!" I didn't get a hit during the entire year, so I was never surprised to hear those familiar words. Oh, if only we could have had a group gardening project instead, or even bike races! But I had decided I should (with emphasis on should!) play baseball. And, in baseball, nobody contradicted the umpire. He ruled!

What about our daily walk with Jesus? For me, a lot of things try to rule my mind — for example, that nebulous feeling of "I'm just not up to it today." Other times it's discouragement, shame, guilt, or anger that my mind gets stuck in. It's kind of like being in a huge vat full of the sticky glue of fear and hesitation, and trying to break free of it. Can you identify?

Colossians 3:15 urges us to let the peace of Christ rule in our hearts. There's a fabulous definition of the Greek word for "rule" in my concordance, which says it means to "act as umpire, be enthroned

as decider of everything." So, when Colossians says let Christ's peace rule, it means rule! If fear takes top position in your mind and starts running the show, then picture the referee (Jesus Christ) running up to you and declaring, "You're safe! You've got peace!"

Have you ever seen basketball coach Bob Knight protest a referee's call against his team? Sometimes our minds can protest just as adamantly, saying, "Peace!? No way! Are you sleep-walking, ref?" If that happens, then just tell your mind that the Prince of Peace is not only the ultimate umpire, but also King, and he knows what he's talking about!

Thankfully, as we let the peace of Christ rule, that glue of fear loses much of its power to bind us, and ever-increasing faith takes its place. Jesus Christ has gone "through the glue" and every other temptation, emerging into victory! He's always there to help us!

Thought for the day: God, whenever the voices of fear, discouragement, or confusion try to rule my mind, help me see that the Lord Jesus Christ has the ultimate authority to declare once and for all, "Peace!"

69. *Ministers of the Love of God*
by Tommy Chittenden

Today's scripture: Ephesians 2:10

When I look at the people around me, I see many wonderful gift-ings and talents. Some are natural givers — benevolent and gener-ous. Some are natural servants — gracious and selfless. Some are natural musicians — playing or singing and bringing great joy and comfort to the hearts of men and women. Some are natural artists — capturing on canvas a picture that transports those who see it to the very instant it was created.

Still others seem naturally gifted in a corporate setting — wheeling and dealing as if they had been created for such a purpose. Others seem just as naturally gifted in a blue-collar setting — with skilled hands at a construction site. Consider the physicians who seem created for just exactly what they do and nurses and other caregivers whose gifts seem to flow from some unseen pool of re-sources that turns them into ministering naturals. If we simply look around, we will see majestic strokes of God's creative hands in each person.

Scripture teaches that we were created in Christ Jesus for good works. Every gifting I just mentioned is a good work. The Word also says, "For in him all things in heaven and on earth were created, things visible and invisible, whether thrones or dominions or rulers or powers; all things were created through him and for him" (Colossians 1:16). Even though we see an endless array of talents and gifts — even though some of those gifts may seem obscure or nonspiritual — all are of equal importance in God's economy. If God was willing to take the time to make each person unique, it stands to reason that God would also have a unique purpose for each and every one of us.

What about it? Consider your own life in this moment. Do you absolutely love who you are and what you do? How would you answer the question, "Do you know who you really are, and are you living your life's passion in what you do every day?"

You and I were created to minister the love of God through the conduit of our individual lives. When we accept this truth, and then accept the giftings of one another, God's creativity will know no boundaries. One gift used in combination with the next and the next and the next brings glory to God and releases the awesome power of the Holy Spirit. This is the ultimate purpose for all — to remember who we are and then think, feel, and act in that awareness, living from the passion of our hearts in whatever we do — bringing glory to our Creator.

Thought for the day: Meditate on the fact that you are the only expression of you that ever was or ever will be created — created to "be Love." So be it!

70. *People Who Need People*
by Tyler Connoley

Today's scripture: Genesis 2:18–24

When people try to use Genesis 2 as a reason for denying the validity of my same-sex marriage, I often wonder, "When was the last time you read Genesis?" Because, when I read that story, I find it says just the opposite of what they think it says.

In Genesis 2, God has created the first human (Hebrew *adam*). The *adam* is called "he" because Hebrew doesn't have a pronoun "it" — all Hebrew nouns are either male or female like in Spanish and French. However, the earliest Rabbis who interpreted this text told us the *adam* was neither male nor female, because God had not created the sexes yet. One image of the *adam* that I really like is of a creature with four arms, four legs, and two heads, similar to the image of the first humans in the Greek myth told by Plato.

God is happy with the *adam*, but realizes the *adam* is lonely. God says, "It is not right for the *adam* to be alone; I will make a helper corresponding to it" (Genesis 2:18, my translation). Then God proceeds to make all the animals of the earth, the birds of the air, and everything that swims in the sea. With each, God brings the animal to the *adam*, who gives it a name, but the text tells us "there was not found a helper corresponding to it" (Genesis 2:20, my translation).

I imagine the story this way, God brings the cat to the *adam* and says, "Will this be a helper corresponding to you?"

The *adam* says, "That's a cat." It loves the way the cat purrs when it's petted, and the way it curls up next to the *adam* when they sleep. The cat is a great stress-reliever and a wonderful companion when the *adam* is sitting under a tree thinking, but the cat is not a helper corresponding to it.

So God brings another animal. And another. They all have nice attributes, but none are quite right.

When all the animals have been made, and a helper corresponding to the *adam* hasn't been found, God puts the *adam* to sleep, and takes one of its sides (the King James Version translates this as "rib," but "side" is closer to the Hebrew meaning). Out of that side, God makes another *adam*/human.

When the *adam* awakes, God brings the new human to it, and this time the *adam* exclaims, "This one, at last, is it! Bone of my bones and flesh of my flesh" (Genesis 2:23, my translation). The *adam* has found a helper corresponding to it and decides to call the new human "woman." Anyone who has fallen in love knows the feeling expressed in that exclamation, *"This one, at last, is it!"*

The message of Genesis 2 is that humans need human companionship. Dogs and cats are great companions, and it's wonderful to commune with nature, but they can never offer the kind of companionship other humans give us. Even if we're not partnered, we are all "people who need people."

Yet some religious conservatives will use Genesis 2 to argue that certain classes of people are to be denied the companionship of marriage, because they fall in love with the wrong person. Arguing that Genesis 2 is all about the sex of the two humans, they say homosexuals must remain celibate for life. Worse yet, families and friends take this message and think it means they must disown their children, brothers, sisters, or friends. Having already denied them the companionship of marriage, they deny LGBTQ people the companionship of community.

Thought for the day: God said, "It is not right for the human to be alone." God's Word has been twisted with the added words "unless you're gay — then you must be alone."

71. *Whom Do You Trust?*
by Deb Doty

Today's scripture: Psalm 20

Back in the days when the psalms were being written, there were many wars between nations (much like today, I guess!). Kings amassed mighty armies designed to defeat their enemies. The more horses and chariots they had, the better their chances were of being victorious. So kings constantly added artillery, putting their trust in their weapons to see them through any challenge. They were proud of their resources and depended on them.

But the writer of this psalm — none other than the mighty warrior, King David — put his trust elsewhere. He put his trust in the name of the Lord. Sure, he had horses and chariots. But his trust wasn't in his arsenal — it was in God. He was proud of God.

It may be hard for us to chunk this down to our time, to our lives. We may be tempted to compare this to the war in Iraq, but you and I aren't the "kings" in charge of that war, and we'd have to speculate on an awful lot. But I believe that you and I are "kings" over the

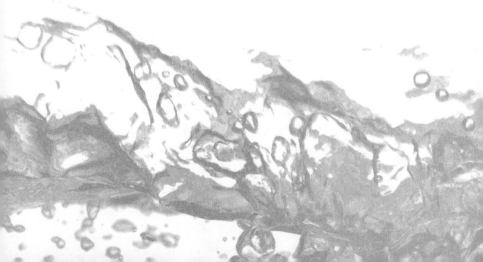

everyday battles we encounter in our lives. And I believe that God has something important to ask us.

What do you put your trust in? What are you proud of? To what do you turn when your back's against the wall? Do you trust in your intelligence to out-think your adversary? Are you proud of your good income that can buy your way out of the mess? Do you rely on your power and influence? Your good looks? Your clique of friends? Your family? All of the above? Or do you trust in God?

When I ask if you trust in God, I don't mean, "Do you trust in your church, your pastor, the deacons, the teachers, or the small-group leaders?" None of these is God. Like horses and chariots, these can fail. But there is One who will bring true, lasting victory. Let's be proud of God; let's trust in God.

Thought for the day: Think about what you rely on most. How can you rely on God more than you trust in that thing or person?

72. *Conformed or Transformed?*
by Pam Beutler

Today's scripture: Romans 12:1–2

Let the same mind be in you that was in Christ Jesus.
(Philippians 2:5)

As a young child in a parochial school, the good sisters of the Blessed Virgin Mary taught us that, when unpleasantries come our way, we should offer our small struggles to Our Lord. We were told that we wouldn't always find an easy way out, but we should offer ourselves to God for his purposes.

Over the years, I realized how I had incorporated this simple lesson into my life. I try to remind myself often that I am here for a bigger cause. I may not have all the luxuries that the 21st century offers, but I have joy and love surrounding me everyday. I try not to let material things weigh me down, and strive to keep my focus on God's purpose for me. I learned as a child to thank God every day for my life and things that God has brought into it, good or bad. I try always to be amazed at God's everyday miracles — a sunrise or

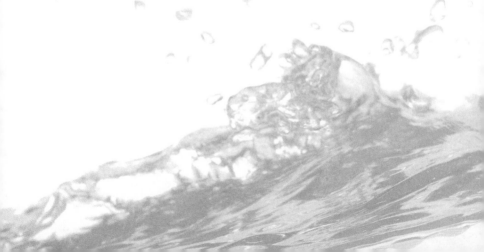

a sunset, the smell of a spring field, or the fury of an Indiana thunderstorm. I often take a moment to clear my mind from the bustle of life and have my conversation with God.

Many of us are bruised souls, making it through this world and waiting for the next life. I know there is more. Each day I give to God my breath, the pain in my joints, the laugh in my belly. When life overwhelms me, and it often does, I stop and pray. I give my life to the One who made me. I ask God to help me look beyond what is taking place. Spiritual transformation through learning is a continuing process.

Thought for the day: What would it mean for me to give this moment to God?

73. *The Fullness of God*
by Kay Olry

Today's scripture: Ephesians 3:16–21

I remember when I first started reading scripture seriously, and coming across this prayer from Paul to the church at Ephesus. It was so different from much of the scripture that I was familiar with. This passage talked about the immensity of love that God has for God's people, and for those who love God.

Many of us have known persons who live their lives in fear or, as Thoreau said, "quiet desperation." People who have never been able to believe in a Creator who loves them as they are keep trying to find the one person, thing, or substance that will fill the hole that can only truly be filled by the Spirit.

When I was in my early twenties, I was out one night in a bar, doing my best to drink away my troubles from the week. I was just beginning to understand my sexuality and the ramifications of being LGBTQ in a straight world. I had decided that if the world wanted to treat me as an outcast, I'd show the world how outcast I could be.

I tried to strike up a conversation with an attractive woman who, quite honestly, didn't want to engage in a conversation with my drunken self. She did manage to tell me where she went to school, Taylor University. I remember being surprised that any LGBTQ person would choose to attend a Christian university. I asked her, "Isn't being gay and Christian a contradiction in terms?" I've never forgotten her simple response: "No, it isn't." That was all she said, and then she walked away. She didn't feel called to explain or justify her response; sometimes, I wish she had.

It took me another six years before I was able to rebuild my own relationship with Christ. I wasted a lot of time. I was in the Air Force for much of it, traveling around the world from Sicily to the Philippines. Every so often, my mind would try to figure out how she was able to integrate her sexuality with her Christianity. What I was really wondering was, how could I? How did she reconcile these two seemingly diametrically opposed tenets? I had heard so many Christians say that God wasn't interested in knowing me unless I changed or chose celibacy. The Air Force would have thrown me out or put me in jail, if they had found out. In the Catholic Church, where I was raised, they were very clear on how they felt about people like me.

Eventually I was able to see God differently, with the help of a retreat I attended, which was sponsored by Catholics no less. God eventually succeeded in calling me back to my faith. It was prayers and scriptures like today's passage that helped me to understand "what is the breadth and length and height and depth, and to know the love of Christ that surpasses knowledge" (verse 18b and 19a). I realized that, regardless of what other people told me, Christ was telling me something else — and that he loved me, too.

I often wondered what happened to that woman in the bar — what she's doing today, what she's become. What a gift she was given to have her head on that "straight" so early (pun intended).

Is there anyone in your life telling you that you aren't "good enough" for a relationship with God? Don't believe them! Don't lose years wondering how to integrate your whole life with Christ and the Church. Take him at his word. Christ invites each of us into relationship, assuring us that Perfect Love is ours, too.

Along with Paul, it is my fervent prayer "that you may be filled with all the fullness of God" (verse 19b).

> **Thought for the day:** In what ways do I need to feel the enveloping love of God? Do I believe that the promises are for me, too?

74. The Deep End
by Robert Ferguson

Today's scripture: Psalm 113

I knew there was going to be a problem. Just a few months ago, my partner and I took the kids to Cedar Point amusement park in Ohio for a water adventure vacation. There would be a full day spent at the water park and at least a full day dedicated to the pool at the hotel. We intended to swim to our hearts' content.

As we set out for our first big splash in the hotel pool, I remembered the problem. Bryce, my seven year old, has no concept of fear of the water. He believes he is a fish. So, unlike his dear old godfather, he does not check little things like water depth! When he sees water, he simply starts running and jumps in. The problem is that Bryce cannot swim. He believes he can swim, and he does a mean dog paddle and splashes around, but it's not swimming. I have had to rescue him from a water emergency on more than one occasion.

So here he is, once again, bolting for the deep end — and I am fully dressed in street clothes. This was supposed to be the kids taking a quick dip before dinner after a long car ride, and the adults were just going to watch from a distance. I tried to stop him, but the series of events was already in play.

Running, jumping, and squealing, he goes headlong into the pool. I am looking right at him when he realizes he can't touch the bottom of the pool, and so begins the furious flailing of arms and the desperate gasps for breath. (Note that in addition to being a world-class dog paddler, Bryce could also be an award-winning dramatic actor.) So now the question for both the eagle-eyed lifeguard on duty and me is this: Is he actually drowning or being gloriously over dramatic? Either way, I have no choice but to jump in, jeans and all, and pull him to safety. He responds with gleeful cheers and requests to do it again!

As I was reading today's passage I was particularly struck by verses 5 and 6. "Who is like the Lord our God, who is seated on high, who looks far down on the heavens and the earth?" The author of the psalm suggests that God's glory is not only high above the heavens and reigning over creation, but our Creator comes down to behold the things of the earth.

The imagery of a God who is not above it all but is concerned for each one of us is comforting. We should all be surprised by the fact that such an awesome and infinite being would have anything at all to do with us. The Creator God actually wants to be involved with the lowly creation.

Our heavenly Parent is watchful over us when we find ourselves in deep water and unable to touch the bottom. We see examples of God's personal involvement throughout the Bible. Shadrach, Meshach, and Abednego were not saved from the fiery furnace; they were saved in the midst of the fiery furnace. Paul and Silas were not saved from the prison; they were saved while behind locked doors in the prison. Daniel was not saved *from* the lions' den, but rather saved *in* the lions' den.

Today we are called to trust and believe that in all times — both good and bad — God is able not only to rescue us, but to raise us to new heights and new places. It is amazing what One so high does for one so low!

Thought for the day: God, thank you for stooping down to be with me. Thank you for the times you've rescued me. Help me to see you and to trust you when I'm in my own deep water.

75. *Vindicate Me, O God!*
by Jeff Miner

Today's scripture: Psalm 43

When I read passages like Psalm 43, where the Psalmist asks God to be defended from "ungodly" oppressors, I get a little uneasy. I remember back to my fundamentalist days and how we took so much comfort in these passages. People often disliked us and said we were judgmental and mean-spirited. We reflexively dismissed their criticism as unjustified, and called out to God to protect us from these "heathens." We engaged in no meaningful introspection. Criticisms were automatically dismissed. After all, we were righteous, so if someone was criticizing us, that person must be unrighteous.

I've seen many times when people of faith are too quick to dismiss criticism and call for God to vindicate them. Before I became a pastor, I oversaw a group of attorneys who regulated savings banks in a bureau of the U.S. Department of Treasury in Washington, D.C. A secretary assigned to support our group was a devout Christian, with Bible verses plastered all over her cubicle. Let's call her "Marsha." She would often respond to something by saying, "Praise the Lord."

Marsha was very sincere in her faith, but she was a bear to work with. She was temperamental, spent too much time on the phone, and aimed mostly to please me (group leader and fellow Christian), while having little regard for the needs of our staff attorneys. One day I heard her out in the hall shouting. When I went to investigate, I discovered that one of our attorneys had asked where a certain project stood and justifiably expressed concern that it wasn't yet done. Marsha went off on the attorney with volcanic anger.

I'm sure Marsha went home that night convinced she was being persecuted, praying and trusting that God would vindicate her.

All of which makes me think about myself. How many times have I asked God to defend me when, in reality, it's others who needed to be defended against me? In other words, how can I objectively distinguish situations where I'm being falsely accused from those where I'm being justifiably criticized?

I believe we find the answer in verse 3, where the Psalmist prays, "O send out your light and your truth; let them lead me." That is a vital prayer. David, who wrote many of the psalms, was known for carefully examining himself before ever dismissing the criticism of an enemy (See 2 Samuel 16:5–14).

We should follow his example. Whenever someone accuses us, we should resist the impulse to reflexively reject the criticism. Instead we should ask God for discernment. After a searching self-examination, we may actually conclude that we've been wrong, in which case we should apologize. Only after we've conducted this self-examination and concluded we're truly innocent can we confidently rest in the assurance that God will defend us.

> **Thought for the day:** We Christians need a lot more humility. We should always double-check to make sure we're on the right side of an issue before invoking God's defense. Only then can we be confident of God's protection.

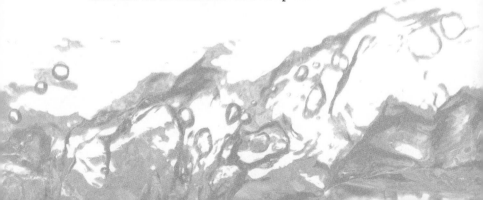

76. Our To-Do List
by Julie Walsh

Today's scripture: 1 Thessalonians 4:13–18

I am always stunned by death. It stops me in my tracks. I have been stung by the news of the tragic death of one of our church members.

I am just stuck today. Every 20 minutes I obsessively check the news web sites seeking more information, searching for clues, looking to make sense of this, hoping that someone will take it all back because I just can't believe what I am reading.

This gentle-spirited man could never have known that this day would be his last. There was too much on his to-do list. His work was probably spread out all over his desk, waiting for another day to get it all done. Dishes and laundry may have been piled up. Was the bed made? Did he make that important phone call?

This tragedy serves as another piercing reminder that life is precious.

I have always carried a naive notion that when it's time to die, our papers will be neatly stacked and filed away, our homes will be tidy, we will be wearing clean underwear, and we will have checked everything off our to-do lists.

But our to-do lists will never be done to our satisfaction. Today I am re-prioritizing my list — again. The paperwork, the dishes, the errands, and the over-busy hum of activity have now been shuffled behind laughter, gratitude, gentleness, forgiveness, and love.

As I allow myself to grieve this loss, I also remember the promise of resurrection offered by Jesus Christ, our Lord. It is with this hope that I recommit myself to righteous living and to the wonderful joy that I find in our salvation.

Thought for the day: Allow yourself to grieve. Remember the resurrection. Live life with hope and love.

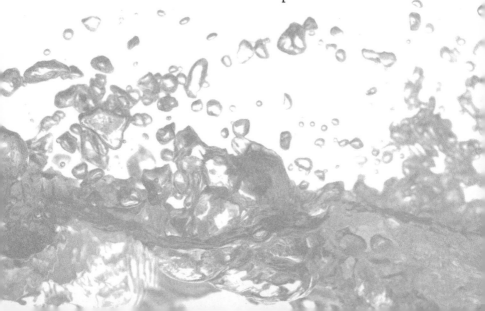

77. Be Strong and Courageous!
by Melody Merida

Today's scripture: Joshua 1:1–9

Now that Moses has died, the people of Israel — who have been wandering in the desert for the past 39 years — need a new leader to guide the way as they prepare to enter the Promised Land. Joshua, Moses' right-hand man, is the guy God chooses for the job.

Here we read what sounds like an incredible list of gifts God is about to bestow upon the Israelite people. The people are set to inherit land as far as the eye can see, no one will be able to stand up against them, and God will never leave them! Those are some remarkable gifts!

It would be easy to read these verses and get the impression that God is making these promises so that the road ahead will be smooth. After all, this sounds pretty rosy, doesn't it? What a sweet deal the Israelite people get. And, hey, they deserve a smooth ride after all of these years spent in the desert, with no place to call home. They've earned it — after all, they're God's chosen people.

But I don't think a free ride is exactly what God is promising. Indeed, the rest of the book of Joshua is a litany of wars and struggles that the Israelites must face as they seek to claim the land God had promised to them. This wasn't a free ride at all. They had to fight for

everything that God had promised to give to them. And fight they did, over and over again.

So did God not keep God's end of the bargain? Did God let the Israelites down?

God didn't promise it would be easy, but God did promise them victory in the end. Three times in this passage — in verses 6, 7, and 9 — God tells Joshua to be strong and courageous. What need is there for courage if difficult times are not ahead? What need is there for strength if that strength will not be tested? The most telling part of the message God gives to Joshua is found at the end of verse 9: "for the Lord your God will be with you wherever you go." That seems to be the key. Joshua could be strong and courageous, because God promised to be with him wherever he went!

Just like Joshua, we've never been promised that our journeys will be easy. God never promised that we would get to detour around all the hardships of life. But God does promise that when we face those battles, God will be there with us.

Thought for the day: The promises of God were true for Joshua, and they are still true for us. Be strong and courageous!

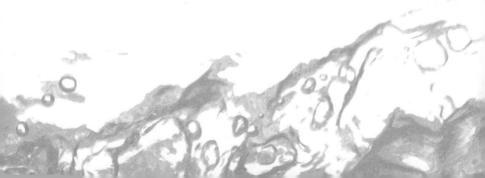

78. On the Right Track
by Robert Ferguson

Today's scripture: Proverbs 3:21–26

Our scripture today focuses on instructions for living a peaceful, Godly life. We are encouraged to always keep and use sound judgment and discernment. Discernment is allowing the Holy Spirit to lead, guide, and direct our paths. We are told that to cherish and celebrate these traits will lead to long abundant life. The text admonishes us to keep these things in view and to not lose sight.

It seems so easy to become distracted by things that are not of God. One of my biggest personal struggles is worry. Many people see me as a happy-go-lucky guy who isn't rattled by much. The truth is I worry a lot. I worry about my job, my car, my family, my health, and my future. There are times when sleep eludes me. It's as if, when I lay my head down to rest, my brain begins to shift into overdrive. Perhaps you've felt the same.

But Proverbs 3 tells us that, if we keep our minds trained on the things of God, then our sleep will be peaceful and our worries will

seem unimportant. I have learned that my worry will not change the outcome of a particular situation. Learning from mistakes and asking God for guidance is a much better way to see results.

We have been given the tools to compete and win in this world. All good tools need continually to be sharpened. How do we keep our tools of sound judgment and discernment sharp? We must stay close to God and continually train ourselves to hear God. When we begin each day with the study of scripture and prayer, we are training our hearts and minds to stay focused on the things of God.

It is easy to lose sight of what is important in this life. Staying in touch with God's Word through study and prayer helps us to stay focused and on the right track.

Thought for the day: God will keep me safe by guiding my way.

79. *Good Shepherd*
by Christen Peters

Today's scripture: John 10:27–29

According to one estimate, 6,515,836,051 people existed in the world at 11:09 a.m. on Sunday, May 14, 2006. I am one, and only one, of them.

And God knows me. God knows my name. Just as Jesus was able to call to Zacchaeus by name in Luke 19:5, you and I are known to God by name. How precious we must be!

Think about the people who pass through your life. I'll bet there are lots of them. Maybe you see them every day, maybe you see them in the halls at work, or the aisles of the grocery store. How many of them do you really know? How many of them do you even know by name? Generally, we know by name the people who have most affected us. What an impression we must have made on God's heart that we are known — each and every one of us.

"But, wait!" you say, "I'm a sinner. In fact, I'm a bad sinner. I've wandered away from God more times than I can count. Surely God is ready for me to go once and for all."

Not even close. God will never let you go for good. In Luke 15, the Pharisees are throwing a fit over Jesus' inclusion of "sinners." Jesus explains that it is the lost sheep who have his full attention. "There will be more joy in heaven over one sinner who repents than over ninety-nine righteous persons who need no repentance" (Luke 15:7). That means you . . . and me . . . and all of the rest of this human fold to which we belong.

That still, small voice that tugs at you when you are wandering away is Jesus calling to you — the Shepherd seeking his precious sheep. He is calling out, "I love you. Come home."

Thought for the day: My God knows me and loves me. And I can never wander so far away that I can't come home.

80. Under Construction
by Julie Walsh

Today's scripture: John 15:1–5

Rolling down the road for hours at a time provides me with a lot of time to think, reflect, contemplate, and absorb visually the abundance of life and creation that surrounds me.

Consider my recent reflection on road construction. I have seen two different methods used to patch holes in the road.

In the first method, the construction crew simply fills the hole with asphalt and pats it down so it is even with the existing pavement, scraping away any of the excess. This method serves as a viable temporary solution, but the filler eventually wears away leaving an exposed hole in the road once again.

In the second method, the construction crew cuts away the pavement surrounding the original hole, making an even larger hole than when they started. With this expanded surface area, the crew

then meticulously works to remove the uneven debris, making a new smooth surface ready for its permanent patch and repair. The entire road is not eliminated, yet this section is replaced with new material to give it better strength and durability.

God, our personal construction manager, continues to carefully shape us, mold us, and prune us. In order to successfully achieve this, circumstances sometimes have to get worse before they can get better. De[con]struction happens before Reconstruction can begin. Walls need to be torn down. Old ways of doing things need to be replaced with new. Pride needs to be replaced with humility. Self-actualization and hard truths must be discovered.

Thought for the day: Don't worry; God will fill all of those empty holes. Remember, you are under construction!

81. *The Peace of God*
by David Zier

Today's scripture: Philippians 4:4–7

This is one of my favorite passages in the Bible because it gives me a sense of peace.

Sometimes — maybe more often than I'd like to admit — I can be very negative, and not have a very positive attitude about things, whether it is about myself, others, or a particular situation. Sometimes I think I'm not good enough for something, I can question why God blesses me when others are more deserving, or I can talk negatively about others and come across as if I think I am the most righteous and perfect person. When I do these things, I don't feel good about myself, and it brings me down even more. When I fill myself up with these things, the peace of God seems to be even farther away.

I love the message of today's passage from Philippians, because I know when I fill my heart, mind, and spirit with praises to God and live my life as a prayer of praise to God, the peace of God consumes me. When I replace the negative with praise, when I lift up those around me for the blessings and gifts God has given them, and when I accept that God has created me for a purpose, I can replace the worry and negative attitudes in my life with a peace of God that surrounds me and fills me.

Consider these words from verses 6 and 7: "The Lord is near. Do not worry about anything, but in everything by prayer and supplication with thanksgiving let your requests be made known to God. And the peace of God, which surpasses all understanding, will guard your hearts and minds in Christ Jesus."

Thought for the day: Are you allowing yourself to live in the peace of God?

82. *Klutzes on Ice*
by Deb Doty

Today's scripture: Galatians 6:1–18

Have you ever walked across a parking lot on a frosty evening, hurrying to your car, eager to escape the wind? You notice your boots leave a fresh path in the snow dust as you scurry across the last few feet to your car. You're fumbling in your pocket with your gloved hands to find your keys when . . . BAM! Suddenly another part of your anatomy is making an impression in the snow.

It's too late, but you notice the patchy black ice and its crazy quilt pattern peeking out here and there from under the snow. If you'd only stepped an inch to the right, you wouldn't be sitting in the middle of a parking lot feeling foolish. But you made a false step.

The Greek word translated "transgression" or "sin" in verse 1 could also be translated "false step." Isn't sin like that sometimes? You're walking along, feeling fine, everything's under control, and BAM! Suddenly you've taken a tumble. It was that doggone false step on the ice. If only . . .

Any one of us can take a false step at any time and land on our backside. When we think we're immune, we're walking across that icy parking lot in the dark with sunglasses on. It's almost a sure thing we won't see the ice until we suddenly see it up close and personal — and painfully so.

Because even the most sure-footed of us can fall, it isn't unusual to come across folks sitting in the parking lot, wondering how on earth they will ever get back to their feet with all the hidden ice just waiting to bring them back down. That's when we must fight the urge to lecture them about being more careful. Instead, we go over and help them up, being careful not to fall ourselves. When we remember our pain and realize our vulnerability, we will be gentle with them. And together we'll make it to our cars.

Thought for the day: Don't leave someone sitting in the cold — help that person up!

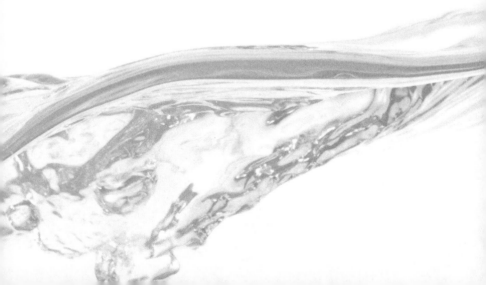

83. *Pierced with a Sword*
by David Zier

Today's scripture: Matthew 10:34–39

I engaged in the practice of *lectio divina* on the book of Matthew recently for some seminary work in a class at the Earlham School of Religion. *Lectio divina* allows you to take in the words of scripture and imagine yourself in the midst of them. The words are read slowly, multiple times, with silence in between, and you imagine you are there "within" the text. As the words are spoken or read, it allows you to feel and be present in the scene. The Spirit can take our minds to a place where the meaning is new and different, yet delivers a strong message about what it means to follow Christ.

These are very difficult words in this passage. How could these words be heard and understood when meditated on by the leading of God? I am surprised that Jesus says he is not here to bring peace, as most would think Jesus wants peace and he is a peaceful man — he's the Prince of Peace!

I think that peace implies contentment. I don't think Jesus wants me to be content, or at peace about what is happening to God's people in the world. Following Jesus is not about being at peace, but about shaking me to my core.

That sharp sword piercing my soul stirs me up and does not allow me to settle for what is less than God's will. It's how Jesus calls me into action.

When there is no justice or peace, he wants to shake me up — he wants me to speak up and take action where people are oppressed, unloved, poor, and do not have a voice. The sword is symbolic of the sharp message of Jesus, a message that pierces the soul. Even though these words may seem harsh, these words should stir the soul — and renew our call to discipleship.

Thought for the day: How has Jesus' message pierced your soul?

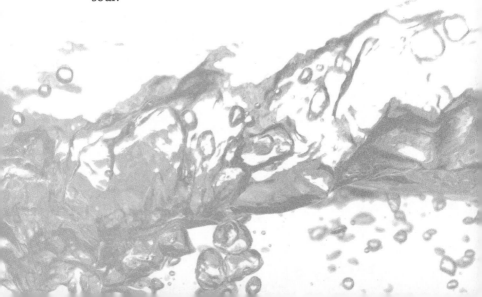

84. And in Summary . . .
by Ben Lamb

Today's scripture: Psalm 19:14

This verse is a pretty keen summary for living a Christian life.

"Let the words of my mouth . . ."

Our actions — including our words — are the acid test of whether or not we're actually following Jesus. Not everyone is a drum major with super-high visibility at all times, but we're all in the Jesus band for the whole world to see.

". . . and the meditation of my heart . . ."

Our actions are strongly influenced by what we're thinking (meditating on) in our lives. When I'm feeling out of sync with Jesus' way of living, it's often because of the type of thoughts I've allowed myself to hang onto.

". . . be acceptable to you, . . ."

Sure, there are plenty of times when I wish God couldn't read my heart's "meditations." (Oh, alright — grumbling, complaining, mean wishes, raunchy thoughts, and so much more.) But you know what? The Christian walk is precisely that: a walk, or a journey, through this world as we get closer to heaven every day. I'm not going to waste time by wallowing in an "I can't be perfect, so I won't try at all" attitude when I stumble along the way. Jesus never decreed a three-strikes-and-you're-out clause for his followers.

". . . O Lord, my rock, and my redeemer."

It never ceases to amaze me how so much of the Old Testament points toward the New Testament. This passage could easily pass as a quotation from a follower of Jesus. He truly is the foundation upon which our lives are based. When I aim to put this into practice because of gratitude for what he already has done for me, it becomes easier than trying to force myself to do it mechanically as a means of "fire insurance."

Conveniently, Jesus' words and meditations of his heart are preserved for us in the Bible. I'm convinced it's perfectly safe to believe that Jesus is pleased when we "plagiarize" his words for use as words coming out of our own mouths and for being instilled upon our own hearts.

Thought for the day: When trying to figure out the way to please God, Jesus' example — as recorded in the Gospels — makes for an "open book" test.

85. *The Promise of Persecution*
by Morgan Stewart

Today's scripture: 2 Timothy 3:10–12

Being a trailblazer in a career dominated by men has not been easy. Years ago, my company affirmed my computer-technology and leadership abilities by promoting me to senior management at the tender age of 29. The newly created position came with executive dining room privileges — a first for any woman at the firm.

Not long after, I entered the formal oak dining room of the prestigious company only to have the maitre d' say, "Miss, this dining room is for use by executives only."

Smirking because such incidents have happened before, I quickly replied, "I am the executive." But the headwaiter, now angry, persisted, "Look, this dining room is only for senior management — not junior associates, assistants, or anyone else!"

Thinking surely I had him this time, again I insisted, "I am the senior manager." But the stubborn man would not budge. Sneering at me over the top of his reservations book, he paged the dining room manager over the public address system, all the while leaving me waiting and others behind me fuming.

I was embarrassed and hurt that another employee would treat me with such contempt. With tears stinging my eyes, I started to walk away, leaving my appetite for lunch and collegiality at the door. Silently, I thought, "Could God really have called me to such a place?" Soon God reminded me of the Bible verse "Be strong in the Lord and in the strength of the Lord's power" (Ephesians 6:10). I decided to stay. As I waited patiently, the restaurant manager soon arrived to seat me and even apologized for the rude maitre d'.

While there are many truths given to us in scripture that we are happy to claim, the promise of persecution is never eagerly anticipated. Yet, this too, was promised to those who follow in the footsteps of Christ. This story may seem like a small example compared to, say, the problems faced by the Apostle Paul, but it was painful at the time, and it's made a difference in the way I understand persecution. May we continue to persevere, and to God be the glory as we try to hang on!

> **Thought for the day:** Precious Lord, you, too, were ridiculed and persecuted for your truth. Remind us that, as we suffer, your presence is always with us. Give us courage to speak up when we can, and stamina to endure where we must.

86. *Oh, It's Perfect!*
by Steve Adams

Today's scripture: Psalm 119:96; 2 Timothy 2:15

When I was in grade school, I remember looking forward to summer vacation as a perfect, almost endless time filled with long, sunny, carefree days and warm, lazy nights when I could stay up as late as my heart desired. And, while I did have some good times, they never approached the idealized vision I had in March or April when I looked forward to them.

Every summer, after just a week or two of "heaven on earth" (no school), I would re-learn the same lesson: Life didn't become perfect just because summer vacation had arrived. And when I became an adult, all that silly idealized thinking fell by the wayside, right? Well, not exactly! It seems old habits die hard. Can you identify?

How many times do I subconsciously expect my partner, spouse, family, job, or church to be perfect? Or, if not perfect, then at least mighty close to it? I may say, "Well, I know I can't expect that!" But isn't that what I do expect if I become irritated at my spouse, friend,

or coworker for making a mistake? Maybe I have a bit more of that perfectionistic thinking than I thought! Often those persons in question were doing the best they could (2 Timothy 2:15), or had a good reason why not.

Sometimes we simply miss the mark even when we're really trying. And sometimes the circumstances of life wear down our resolve to put forth our best effort. If so, then Jesus Christ is there to fill us with grace and motivation for tomorrow!

We see glimpses of perfection here on earth, but never the entirety of it. But I think that's good — it helps us see that we absolutely need God. It's at the point when we've done our absolute best, and there's simply no more we can give — and yet things still need improvement — that we can fall into the strong, loving, tender arms of our heavenly Mother/Father, and trust!

> **Thought for the day:** It's only God the Creator, the Lord Jesus Christ, and the Holy Spirit who can give us the perfection we long for.

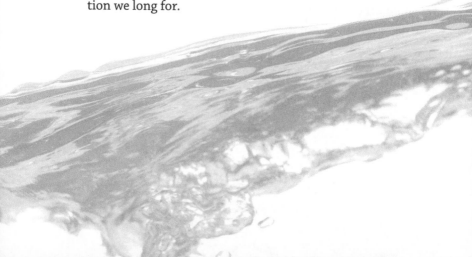

87. *Rejoice in the Lord? Now?!*
by Tyler Connoley

Today's scripture: Habakkuk 3:17–19; Psalm 22:1–5

At first glance, Habakkuk seems crazy. He lists all the things that are going wrong in his life. Most pressing, he's under the threat of impending starvation, because there's no food left anywhere — no grapes, no olives, no sheep for milk or meat. He and his family seem destined to die a terrible death before the season is out. "Yet," he says, "I will rejoice in the Lord" (verse 18a).

How is that possible? How can someone "rejoice in the Lord" when everything has gone wrong? When he's starving? The answer comes from the psalm that Jesus quoted on the cross: *"My God! My God! Why have you forsaken me?"*

For Jesus on the cross, death was not just coming soon, it was imminent. When he said those words, he was suffering from nails in his hands and feet, lash marks on his back, and a crown of thorns on his head. In order to have the voice to say those words, he had to push down on the nail in his feet, hold himself up, and gasp for breath. He was under too much strain to quote the whole psalm, but you can be sure he knew the rest of it.

The writer begins Psalm 22 by stating that he can't see, hear, or feel God. He feels far from God — abandoned. But then he recounts the things God did for his ancestors. He reaffirms his faith in God, not because of his current circumstances, but because of how God has been faithful in the past. He reminds himself that it hasn't always been so bad. And this gives him hope that it won't be bad in the future.

Habakkuk said, "I will exult in the God of my salvation" (verse 18b). Despite his circumstances, he rejoiced in a God who had proven faithful in the past and would prove faithful again. Jesus quoted Psalm 22 as he was dying, and God proved faithful by resurrecting him from the dead.

Thought for the day: Count your blessings. It seems like such a trite idea, and yet it's often exactly what we need to bring us through tough times to the resurrection that waits on the other side.

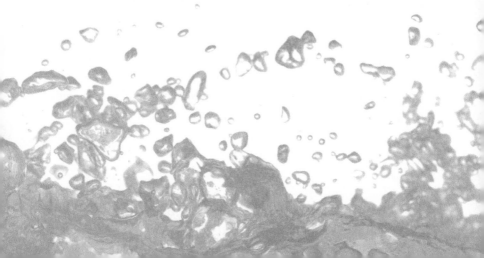

88. What's in Your Hand?
by Deb Doty

Today's scripture: Judges 4:17–24

Jael did what with a tent peg? Eeeeuuuuuuuw! How gross!

Maybe one of the reasons why this passage can offend our modern (and postmodern) sensibilities is that it's a woman who performs the act of extreme violence, skewering a sleeping human being — a human being she has lured into a sense of safety and trust. It's shocking because it's so unexpected. She isn't a warrior. She's a housewife. Besides, she's not even an Israelite. She's a Kenite — this ain't her fight! So how in the world did she end up turning a macho (but exhausted) general into a shish kabob?

Let's pause to take a look at the context. Kenites were the nomadic descendents of Moses' wife's father. They had entered the Promised Land (Canaan) with the Israelites, so their history had intertwined with Israel's history. But our passage tells us that Jael's husband had set off on his own, and his clan was at peace with King Jabin, General Sisera's boss. So it appears that Jael's clan was a neutral party to the war that was taking place between Israel and Canaan.

Picture it: Sisera, exhausted after running from a lost battle, staggers to a tent, seeking haven among a friendly group of people. Jael welcomes him, comforts him, and feeds him — just as you'd expect a Middle Eastern nomadic woman of her time to do. And just as could be expected from a Middle Eastern macho general of his time, he feels safe. He is alone with a mere woman (no threat there!) — and this woman will, of course, follow his orders and protect him. He has nothing to fear, so he falls sound asleep.

The Bible doesn't tell us why Jael decides to do what she does. But for some reason, Jael decides not to be neutral. Maybe something about Israel's God resonates within her heart and she just has to side with that God. Or maybe she's figured out that, if Sisera is running like a frightened hare, it's wisest to side with the obvious winners. But whatever her reason, she chooses to side with Israel.

With that decision made, she makes an even more startling decision. She — a lone woman — will kill the mighty General Sisera. And so she picks up a tent peg and a hammer and tiptoes up to the snoring soldier and . . . BAM! She pins him like an insect in a Boy Scout's bug collection. And from that moment on, the tide turns, Israel subdues King Jabin of Canaan, and Israel lives in peace for 40 years.

By the way, did I mention that part of a nomadic housewife's duties included setting up the tent? Yup, tent pitching was woman's work. So, when Jael decided to kill Sisera, she picked up two familiar household items — items she used with regularity — a tent peg and her hammer. Using what she just happened to have at hand, a woman's tools, she turned the tide for Israel.

Are you in the middle of a battle in your life? Do you cry out to God, "But I can't make a difference! I can't possibly overcome this terrible situation! I've tried and tried, but I still can't seem to defeat this one thing. God, why don't you send someone bigger and stronger than me to set everything right?"

Look around you. What's that in your hand? Only a hammer or a tent peg? Think again.

Thought for the day: Look around with fresh eyes. The very thing you need may be right there in your hand.

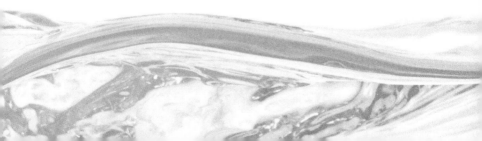

89. *Straight Talk*
by Tyler Connoley

Today's scripture: Matthew 18:15–17

Practically speaking, I probably refer to these verses more than any other passage in the New Testament. Their message is so simple, and yet so useful when dealing with conflicts.

I used to work at a company that made all its employees take a communications seminar once a year. Sometime before I was hired, there had been a big blow up in the company that was caused by what they called "poor communications" (it was really gossip). So, every year, we had to take a seminar in which they taught us the proper way to communicate.

In that seminar, developed by a high-paid consultant, we used puppets to act out situations. We also learned the following rules:

- If you have a problem with someone, go to that person directly.

- If that doesn't work, then (and only then) go to a manager or to Human Resources.

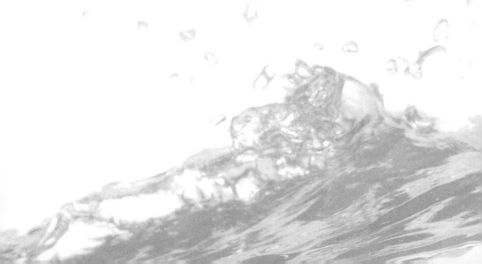

- If someone comes to you with a grievance against someone else, refer that person to Rule #1 and suggest speaking to that person directly.

Do those rules sound familiar? They should, because Jesus gave them to us two thousand years ago. We don't need a high-paid consultant to tell us they work, but we do sometimes need the courage to follow them.

Thought for the day: "If your brother or sister sins against you, go first and point out the fault in private." God, give us the wisdom and courage to follow this simple advice, even in our business life.

90. *Soul Gardening*
by Christen Peters

Today's scripture: Matthew 13:1–9, 18–23

I have always viewed these passages with something of a "that's just the way it is" kind of attitude. Some people will hear and not understand (verses 4 and 19). Some people will be all gung-ho, then fall away the first time the going gets tough (verses 5–6 and 20–21). Some people will hear, but allow worldly matters to distract them (verses 7 and 22). And there are some people who will just plain get it (verses 8 and 23).

I'm led now, though, to consider these passages more as directives for growth than the absolutes I often thought them to be. This is the time of year when I begin working in my own garden, and it's given me a more visual picture of these words.

The first thing I have to do is to work the soil so that it will be receptive to the seeds I will sow. The seed can't even begin to take root if there is no soft place for it to be. In the case of my spiritual garden, this means regularly taking myself to a place that allows me to really learn to understand the Word of God. I open my soul by attending worship services and hearing the words of God explained and by regularly seeking opportunities to learn more.

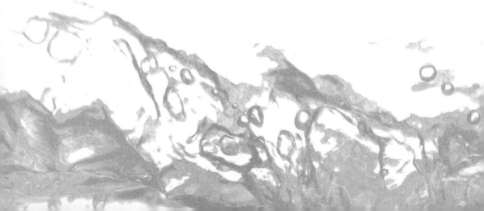

Once the seeds I've planted begin to grow, they still need regular attention. I can't just wipe my brow and walk away. The plants have to be tended with regular watering and feeding for them to grow deep roots. My soul needs the same thing. Daily quiet time — in whatever form that takes — is one of the key ways my soul gets its sustenance.

As grow the plants, of course, so grow the weeds. It is up to me to pull the weeds and protect the plants. The same is true of my soul. The weeds of this world are everywhere I turn — and sometimes I don't recognize that they are draining my time and energy until it is too late. Having a close-knit group of friends to "pluck the weeds" — or at least point them out — is very important. This may be a study group, a ministry team, or a small group. These are the people that see and know me best, the ones who care about the path I'm on and who love me enough to point it out when I begin to lose my focus.

Thought for the day: My soul is my spiritual garden, and it needs regular attention.

91. *God's Testimony Is True*
by Tyler Connoley

Today's scripture: John 5:15–47

Jesus said the works he did testified to the fact he was sent by God. In the face of great opposition from the religious leaders of his day, he was able to stand up straight and say, "There is another who testifies on my behalf, and I know that God's testimony to me is true" (verse 32). The proof of Jesus' sonship was the work God was doing in his life and in the lives of those around him. When I read this passage, I think of what Jesus said in John 14:12: "Very truly, I tell you, the one who believes in me will also do the works that I do and, in fact, will do greater works than these."

Today, we also experience persecution from religious leaders. As far as we know, no one is plotting to crucify the leaders of our church, but modern-day Pharisees certainly stand against us for breaking their rules, just as they persecuted Jesus for healing on the Sabbath. Can we, like Jesus, point to the work God is doing in our lives and say God testifies on our behalf? I think so.

In the last chapter of our book, *The Children Are Free,* Pastor Jeff and I put forth an important argument for the full inclusion of

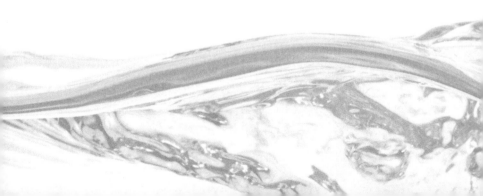

LGBTQ people in God's kingdom, which is essentially the same as what Jesus says in John 5. In the section titled *"You will know them by their fruits,"* we spend several pages chronicling the way God is working in the lives of LGBTQ Christians around the world — from lives transformed to miracles of healing. Then we say, "Everywhere you look, the gift of the Holy Spirit (God's seal of approval) is evident in the lives of gay and lesbian Christians and our worship communities."

> **Thought for the day:** Maybe the opposition of religious conservatives still scares you. If so, think about how God is working in your life. You are a child of God — and, like Jesus, you can say, "I know God's testimony to me is true." And remember to pray for those whom we know are having a hard time believing they are God's children, and that can include ourselves as well. May we listen to God's testimony and really believe what God says to us.

92. *Cloud of Witnesses*
by David Squire

Today's scripture: Hebrews 11:32–40, 12:1–2

It was a Monday morning when my parent's dog died. Savannah, a Rottweiler, was the gentlest, sweetest dog you've ever seen. Mom has a picture of my four-year-old niece asleep with her head resting on Savannah's side. Savannah just kept watch, and didn't move as Mary slept.

This gentle dog had been sick with lymphoma for two and a half years, and it was her time. Mom said that, in the last week, Savannah just hadn't been herself. Though she didn't seem to be in pain, she was tired, and her eyes were different, like the spirit had begun to dim. On that Monday, she ate a little breakfast, went outside for a few minutes, came back into the house, and died.

Mom said that, when Savannah came into the house that last time, she bounced up the steps like her old self, and Mom just happened to be in the right place to see her as she scampered in.

Savannah's death has hit my parents pretty hard — if you have a pet you love, you understand. As I talked to Mom about this the next day, she told me how good it was to see that bit of life, that reminder of her "old self," in Savannah at the very end. She called it a gift from God, and I don't doubt that it was. Mom was also grateful that they didn't have to make the awful decision to have Savannah put down.

Mom was crying as we talked about this (I was, too), but even in her pain her faith was clear — and I'm grateful I got to see that.

Mom's faith has always been an example to me. We've had our disagreements — boy, we've had our disagreements — but I'm blessed beyond measure that I've been nurtured and inspired by such a person of faith. She's part of the "cloud of witnesses" that surrounds me and nourishes my own faith.

> **Thought for the day:** Who's part of your cloud of witnesses? Who inspires your faith? It might be parents, a teacher or pastor, your spouse, or a friend. How can you honor their example today?

93. *One Life to Live*
by Tyler Connoley

Today's scripture: Ecclesiastes 9:7–10

I've always liked Qoholet, the "Teacher" of Ecclesiastes. I appreciate his honesty about the way the world works. He acknowledges that, sometimes, bad things happen to good people, and bad people prosper at the expense of the good. He is a man who tried every pleasure the world had to offer, and found them all vanity, literally "like smoke."

In his book, Qoholet doesn't get bogged down in lofty theology, or preach a prosperity gospel that promises an easy life for the faithful. What he does focus on, what he promises, is that we can enjoy the time we have on this earth if we're willing to accept what God gives us for today. His is a practical book, telling us how to get the most out of a world that often seems unfair and chaotic.

Ecclesiastes 9:7–10 is a pointed reminder to live in the present moment. Consider the words (my translation):

> Go to it then. Eat your food and enjoy it, and drink your wine with a cheerful heart; for God has already accepted what you have done. Always be dressed in white and never fail to anoint your head. Enjoy life with the one you love all the fleeting days of your allotted span here under the sun; for that is your lot while you

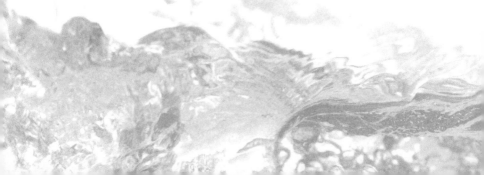

live and labor here under the sun. Whatever work you find to do, do it with strength. For there is nothing of work, explanation, knowledge, or wisdom in the land of the dead where you will go.

These verses are an admonition from someone who has been-there-done-that and finally found the key to real happiness: Enjoy the things you have, instead of worrying about the things you don't have; do what you do well, instead of wishing you had someone else's talent.

The secondary message of this text is just as important: God accepts you as you are. Particularly for those of us who don't conform to society's norms, this can't be said often enough. In a society that expects us all to be straight and gender-conforming, Qoholet says, "God has already accepted what you have done. Always be dressed in white and never fail to anoint your head with oil." Love yourself, because God has already anointed you as a royal heir.

Thought for the day: Qoholet says to eat and drink with joy. Carry yourself with dignity. Love with gusto. And do the best work you can. In short, enjoy the life God gave you, because it's the only one you've got.

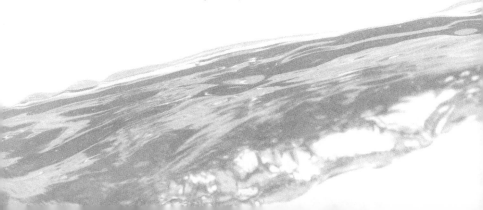

94. *What's in a Name?*
by Mark Shoup

Today's scripture: 1 John 4:4–11

As the closest thing to a receptionist that our church has, it sometimes falls to me to receive and respond to hate-filled emails and phone calls from other Christians who feel it is their duty to marginalize and verbally persecute the members of our church.

These usually don't bother me much, but lately the unusual harshness and sheer volume has begun to wear on me and trouble me even when I'm not at work. What bothers me is not what these people are saying — I really don't value their opinions that much — but rather how someone claiming to be a Christian could be so filled with hate, particularly against another follower of Christ.

It honestly makes me want to not identify myself as a Christian sometimes, because of the bad reputation some have given to that name. I know that as soon as you say you are Christian, some will immediately think, "Oh, like Jerry Falwell, Pat Robertson, and James Dobson!" And I really don't want to be lumped in with that brand of Christianity.

When I'm feeling this way, two things help me restore perspective. The first is scriptures like this one that say opposition to the message of Christ, even from those claiming to speak for God, will happen and is to be expected.

The second is to think about the real, historical Jesus and how he conducted himself. He was not filled with hate, nor did he encourage that kind of attitude in others. His judgment was reserved for those who were persecuting or marginalizing others, not for those simply doing the best they could under their circumstances.

> **Thought for the day:** When you are propagating a message of hope, love, and acceptance, and someone tells you that you are in opposition to what Jesus stood for, that person simply does not know Christ. "Everyone who loves is born of God and knows God."

95. *Save the Children*
by Tyler Connoley

Today's scripture: Leviticus 18:21–23

Probably none of the clobber passages is as terrifying to gay men as Leviticus 18:22. It seems so clear when taken at face value, and gay bashers are always quick to throw it at us with disgust: "it is abomination." But what if I told you that Fred Phelps, one of the most notorious of our contemporary gay bashers, was one of the most prominent violators of that very verse? When read in its historical context, I believe Leviticus 18:22 should strike fear into those who would destroy our queer youth in the name of God.

In unpacking the meaning of Leviticus 18:22, my first question is why women aren't mentioned. If God intended this verse as a condemnation of all same-sex relationships, then wouldn't it make sense to add, "Women, do not lie with womankind as with mankind"? Doesn't this seem like a big oversight if same-sex relationships are so abominable?

The most common response to this is to point out that women are pretty much ignored in the Hebrew Bible. The laws in Leviticus and Deuteronomy were written for the ruling patriarchy and not for

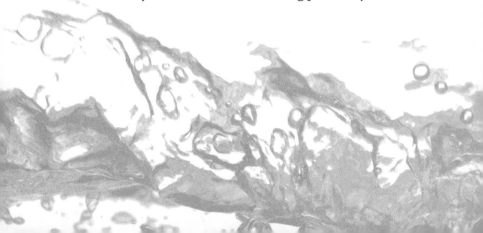

women, people say. However, the very next verse includes women. Leviticus 18:23 prohibits sex with animals and specifically states, "nor shall any woman give herself to an animal to have sexual relations with it" (NRSV). So it looks like the author intentionally left women out of verse 22. But why?

Here we need a little science lesson from 2,000 BCE. In ancient western Asia, where Leviticus was written, people believed semen contained little people. At the time, no one knew about women's eggs, so they thought men provided the children and women provided the incubator. The man would implant the tiny person in the woman's womb, and it would grow there until it was big enough to live on its own. Then it would be born.

Thus, masturbation was thought of as killing one's children before they were born. And offering one's semen to a god was thought of as sacrificing one's children to that god. The most common way this was done was by having sex with the priests who represented a god or goddess.

With this in mind, one possible explanation for the prohibition in Leviticus 18:22 is that it is a prohibition against child sacrifice. God didn't want men having sex with temple priests and thereby offering their children to idols. The context of this verse makes that

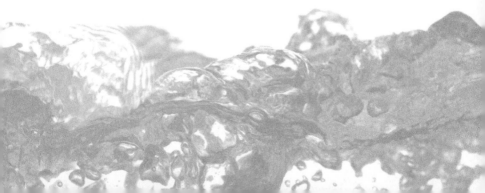

interpretation seem even more likely. Leviticus 18:21 says, "You shall not give any of your offspring to sacrifice them to Molech, and so profane the name of your God: I am the Lord" (NRSV). One of the ways the Canaanites worshipped Molech was by sacrificing their children through burning. Because authors tend to lump items in a list together in groups, it makes sense that this prohibition against child sacrifice would be followed by another prohibition against a different form of child sacrifice.

This leads me to ask, "Do we still sacrifice our children to idols?" And the answer is most definitely, "Yes." We no longer burn our children on altars or have sex with temple priests, but we sacrifice our children in more subtle ways. I know many people whose parents forced them into professions they hated and weren't suited for by threatening to cut them off. Modern people sacrifice their children on the altar of medicine or law, believing a good-paying job is the most important thing in the world.

Other people sacrifice their children to false images of God. My spouse used to serve as the director of Indiana Youth Group, the LGBTQ youth group in Indianapolis. In that job he worked with

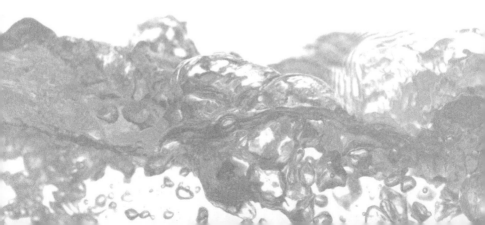

homeless youth and discovered that, although LGBTQ people make up a small percentage of the general population, LGBTQ youth make up between 40 and 60 percent of the homeless youth population. He also found that between 50 and 70 percent of LGBTQ youth have seriously considered suicide — not just thought about it, but planned how and when they would carry it out.

Parents throw their children out of the house in the name of an incorrect reading of Scripture. They abandon their children to hopelessness and suicide, telling them they're an abomination, or force their children into ex-gay therapy programs based on dubious science. Fred Phelps assaults our queer youth with cries of "God hates fags," and God weeps and shouts, "Stop! Have you not read Leviticus 18:22? Stop sacrificing your children to false idols!"

Thought for the day: Don't let Leviticus 18:22 scare you. Instead let it give you a passion for saving our children from being sacrificed.

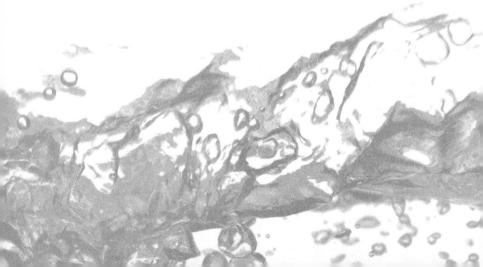

96. *Wings*
by Julie Walsh

Today's scripture: Psalm 91:4–7

It is so easy to withdraw from our friends, family, work, and even church when we feel discouraged or depressed. We want to hide our emotions and barricade our sorrows. How easy it is to go back to bed and pull the covers up over our heads!

We are typically taught by our society that we should not hide from the world — especially in such trying times. (Dr. Phil or Jerry Springer, anyone?) Yet here is God offering us shelter and a place to hide! Take an even closer look, and note that it is under God's wings where we will discover protection and courage.

Reading this psalm brings the lyrics for *Still,* one of our worship songs, to mind:

> *Hide me now under Your wings*
> *Cover me within Your mighty hands*
> *When the oceans rise and thunders roar*
> *I will soar with You above the storm.*
> *Lord, You are the King over the flood.*
> *I will be still and know You're God.*

Are you looking for comfort? Searching for strength? Retreat to the wings of God where you will unconditionally find love, grace, forgiveness, and peace.

Thought for the day: Quiet yourself to receive God's nurture and protection in your storm.

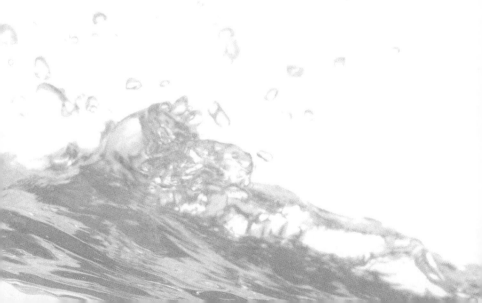

97. *Samurai Warriors*
by Melody Merida

Today's scripture: Psalm 27:1–5

Wow, the beautiful poetry of this passage is astounding! Emerson has nothing on David. I'm moved by the sense of surety that I see in the stanzas of this poem. There is the feeling that no matter what happens, if God is with us, we will prevail.

A few years ago when my nephew Seth was around four years old, we had an afternoon of play time together. Seth loves to play anything — as long as it requires swords! On this particular day, we were playing "samurai warriors," and Seth carried his sword with pride as he strolled around the pretend village he was sworn to protect. Each time I would present him with an adversary about to invade his village, he would make a few quick jabs with his sword, then throw in some punches, kicks, and maybe even a couple of "flips" to escape the enemy. He would fight this way for about two minutes and then declare overwhelming victory. This was the same scenario no matter the number and strength of the enemy invaders.

At the end of our play time I asked him how he alone could manage to defeat all of the enemies. He looked at me as if I were a fool when he said, "I wasn't alone. Didn't you see my sword? Because the sword is so powerful, if I have it, I can win against anybody. It doesn't matter if they're bigger or stronger than me because the sword is stronger than everybody."

I think Seth and David are onto something. With God as our light, salvation, and even our sword, there is nothing that can defeat us. Let that sink in for a moment. What David is saying here — and what little four-year-old Seth seems to have no trouble believing — is that, with incredible power and strength, the victory is assured. Truly, if God is our light and our salvation, what in the world do we have to fear?

> **Thought for the day:** God, teach me to trust in your light and rest in your shelter, knowing that you are able to defeat any "sword" that comes against me. Amen.

98. *The Voice of Truth . . .*
by Kay Olry

Today's scripture: Psalm 138:7

I have two very different voices I hear in my head whenever I have trials and tribulations going on in my life.

The first one is the voice of truth; it tells me that God loves me, wants the best for me, and wants to take care of me. It tells me that, regardless of how I feel about a situation, I can know — because of promises that God makes over and over again in scripture — that, if I just invite God into a situation, God will give me whatever I need to take care of whatever is going on. This voice is the voice of my faith, the voice of truth, and it is where I wish I stayed all of the time.

The other voice is the voice of my fear, doubt, and depression. It tells me that nothing good can come from my bad situation, that everything isn't going to be okay, or that, while God could definitely change things if God wanted to, I often doubt that God will.

I am learning that, when these voices compete for my attention, I can change which one I decide to listen to; notice I said "decide." It becomes an act of will, regardless of feelings, to believe God's word. I've heard that feelings aren't facts — and, in truth, this has been my experience. My prayer is often, "Lord, I believe. Help my unbelief."

The part of my faith that I've been thinking a lot about lately is the presence of the Holy Spirit in my life: Comforter, Counselor, and Friend. Jesus told us before he left that he would send us a Helper. As I grow in my faith, I'm learning that the Holy Spirit is the voice of truth that I'm hearing. That other voice is just me, trying to fight the world on my own, which of course never works. Even when I don't know how to pray, or what to pray for, I can know that the Holy Spirit is helping me more than I can know.

As Romans 8:26 tells us: "Likewise the Spirit helps us in our weakness; for we do not know how to pray as we ought, but that very Spirit intercedes with sighs too deep for words."

Which takes me to something else I've heard before: I can't, God can. . . . I think I'll let God.

Thought for the day: Which of the voices do I listen to?

99. *Nothing in All Creation*
by Jeff Miner

Today's scripture: Romans 8:31–39

As I was growing up, there was no one quite so special as my Grandma Miner. The thought that something might separate me from her love would be unbearable.

Then it happened. I was about seven years old. Dad had borrowed Grandma's car — a 1964 Chevy Impala. Grandma's big blue Impala was much bigger than our little Volkswagen Beetle, especially that huge back seat. My two sisters and I were wound tight, bouncing on the big back seat as Dad drove. Several times he told us to settle down. I was an angel, but my sisters always tempted me into trouble. So there we were, bouncing away when, on one especially good bounce, my head crashed into the ceiling dome light, shattering it.

"Jeff," Dad said, "I warned you! Now you're going to be the one who tells Grandma you broke her car." I sat back in the seat mortified. For all I knew, it would cost thousands to repair Grandma's dome light. I dreaded the thought of telling her. I was evil, terrible, awful! She would probably never love me again.

As we drove up to her house, I figured it would be best to get this over with. I ran into the house. She was sitting in her chair in the living room talking to someone. I threw myself into her lap crying. "Honey," she said, "what's the matter?"

"Grandma," I said, barely able to get out the words, "I broke your dome light!"

I'll never forget her response. Without skipping a beat, she said, "Honey, don't worry about that. We'll just get it fixed." Then she gave me a big hug — a hug I'll never forget, one of the best hugs ever. It was then that I realized that nothing could ever separate me from the love of my Grandma — nothing! What a wonderful, secure feeling!

In today's scripture reading, God is trying to communicate that same feeling to us. "Who will separate us from the love of Christ?" Paul asks. The resounding, liberating answer comes back: Nothing! God's love for you is as deep, and deeper, than my Grandma's love for me. When we do something dreadful and throw ourselves in God's lap confessing, God's response is, "Honey, that's okay. We'll work together to fix it as best we can, and then move on." There are a lot of things we can do to cause pain and destruction in our lives, but there is nothing we can do to separate us from God's love. And "nothing" means "nothing."

> **Thought for the day:** Confess, right now, the thing that you most fear may separate you from God, then picture God's arms surrounding you with everlasting love.

100. *The Greatest Possession*
by Tyler Connoley

Today's scripture: Hebrews 10:32–36

As verse 32 makes clear, the author of Hebrews is talking to people who have suffered great persecution. Those who haven't been abused and persecuted are friends of people who were. I'm reminded of my mother's description of Cambodia: "There is no one here," she said, "who can't tell a tragic story of seeing a family member beaten or murdered." And yet, Mom found the people in Cambodia incredibly happy and friendly — quick to smile and quick to love.

The people in Hebrews 10 and the friends my mother made in Cambodia are proof that what's inside is what matters. The author of Hebrews promises that our confidence will result in a great reward.

This isn't a pie-in-the-sky reward, but the peace, love, and grace that pass all understanding, which are the rewards of those who follow God.

The author says his readers were able to endure "the plundering of your possessions, knowing that you yourselves possessed something better and more lasting" (verse 34b). They held, inside themselves, the Spirit of God and the enlightenment that God brings, even in the toughest circumstances. They knew that what was in them was greater than what was in the world.

> **Thought for the day:** Have you allowed the circumstances of life to take away your smile and your love? Reclaim them as your birthright, as a child of God.

Appendix 1: How to Pray

Prayer is not about a set of rules — it's all about building our relationship with God. It's about conversation, both expressing yourself and listening. Here are some suggestions for making your prayer time effective.

Focus — don't do two things at once.

Multi-tasking is not a virtue when it comes to prayer. Sure, you can pray while you're driving your car (sometimes it's even necessary!), but don't let that be the only time you pray. You can talk to a friend while you're driving; but if they're really a close friend, you will find time to spend with that person when you can just talk and share the joys of having a close friend. It's the same with God.

Get away; find a quiet place where you can unwind and be you.

That might be found in your bedroom or living room, on the back porch, or in the garage. Try something different!

God knows who you are — you don't have to pretend.

Talk about what's on your mind instead of what you think you're supposed to. This is a conversation!

Don't try to impress God (or anyone else) by your eloquence or by using "thee" and "thou" or by being sickeningly sweet, but pray to God as in conversation with a good friend.

Talk out loud. Don't be restricted by posture.

Nowhere does scripture say that prayer must be on one's knees. It may be walking and talking. It may be sitting and talking to the "empty chair," picturing that Jesus is sitting with us as we talk with him.

Make a prayer list or journal for consistency and to track progress.

Develop a list of items for focused prayer. Then review the list at the end of three months and see what has happened. Make adjustment for the next three months.

Suggestions for a prayer list/journal:

- ☑ What is your greatest source of stress right now?
- ☑ What do you fear the most right now?
- ☑ What is the greatest challenge you face over the next three months?
- ☑ What do you need or desire that you don't have now?
- ☑ What change do you need to make in your life?
- ☑ What do you think is the most important thing God wants you to do in the next three months?

It takes discipline to get started, and to stick with it.

Schedule a time during the day for prayer time. Whether it's first thing in the morning or at lunchtime (shutting the office door or going to sit in the car), whether it's first thing when coming home (before fixing dinner or checking messages), or last thing before bed, try to fix a time into your schedule for a week to see how it's working at that given time and to begin to develop a habit.

When you're distracted during prayer time:

- ☑ By random thoughts: Try a "Parking Lot." Have a note pad where you can write down random thoughts so they won't continue to be a distraction. You can come back to them later.

- ☑ If your space is too noisy: Find another place. Some people even go the garage or bathroom to have some uninterrupted peace!

☑ If there's not enough time: Make a date with God. Write it in your planner. You can always find the time to do the things you really want to do.

A Sample "Recipe" for Effective Prayer

Mix and match from these ingredients or others to find the prayer style that works for you.

Some "Conversation Starters"

Begin with singing or listening to a praise song.

Things God wants to hear from you:
☑ What are you afraid of?
☑ What is weighing on you?
☑ What are you excited about?
☑ What's going well?
☑ What are you ashamed of?
☑ What needs to change?
☑ What's the best thing that's happened to you this past week?
☑ What's the worst?
☑ Do you feel like you're going too fast or too slow in life?
☑ What are you especially thankful for this week?
☑ Do you love Me?

Things we want to hear from God:
☑ How do you feel about my past day or week?
☑ Where did I do well?
☑ Where did I fall short?
☑ Do you still love me?

Lift specific requests.

Close with something like this:

"God, I ask you to reveal yourself to me. I want to know your dreams, your hopes, your concerns, your desires. Please reveal yourself to me."

Be alert, listening as you go forward.

Appendix 2: About the Authors

Ben Lamb grew up in the Midwestern part of the United States and attended church(es) all of his life. He has been with Jesus Metropolitan Community Church since 2006. His interests include: music (classical, Carpenters), *I Love Lucy*, auto racing (especially IRL), do-it-yourself projects around the house and yard, and spending quiet evenings with small groups of friends. Ben says, "It is an honor, indeed, to have opportunities to attempt to share God's love with you, the reader of this book. Please share God's love with others in your own life so that they may know it, too."

Brent Walsh was raised in Illinois and home schooled in a conservative Christian family. Upon graduation, he attended Northwest Baptist Bible College in Dunbar, Wisconsin, and, later, Bryan College in Dayton, Tennessee. He has made several trips to South Africa, engaging in dialog with Christians about homosexuality and the Bible. He now serves as a panelist in transgender awareness forums, and he drives over the road with his partner, Julie.

Christen Peters was born in Elwood, Indiana, and has lived in the Hoosier state her whole life. Raised as a Catholic, she says she has always had a contentious relationship with God. Her priests did not adequately answer her big questions on faith, leading her to leave the church. An Indiana University grad in Eastern European history and Russian language and literature, Christen has worked in information technology for 24 years, currently with Community Health Network. Mother of a 17-year-old daughter and owner of four dogs, four cats, and four fish, Christen is interested in photography, history, and arguing about theology. She says she likes Jesus MCC because she has the freedom to ask the hard questions.

David Squire was raised in a conservative Baptist family with five siblings. He serves as Communications Director for Jesus Metropolitan Community Church, and is the editor and coordinator for the *Be Still and Know* online devotional resource. He's been part of the Jesus MCC staff since 1999. Before coming to Jesus MCC, he worked in various technical and creative fields, including web site design  and management, graphic design, and data management. David and his partner, David Wene, have been together since 1997. They were joined in Civil Union in Vermont in December 2000.

David Zier has been an engineer and consultant to the medical device industry for many years, including time at Eli Lilly & Company and the U. S. Food and Drug Administration. In 2007, he began seminary, pursuing a Master of Divinity in Pastoral Ministry at Earlham School of Religion in Richmond, Indiana. David's spouse is Jeff Miner, Senior Pastor of Jesus Metropolitan Community  Church, Indianapolis. They were married September 8, 1990.

Deb Doty has served as the Director of Discipleship at Jesus Metropolitan Community Church since January 2006. Because she serves in this staff position as a volunteer, she earns her living as a program director at a state psychiatric hospital. Deb has extensive experience in human resources, training, management, and writing and editing. She is a graduate of Anderson University and has completed one year at Christian Theological Seminary, Indianapolis. Deb and her spouse, Jenni Clarkson, were joined in Holy Union in December 2003. They live with their wacky Cairn terrier, Andy, and their insane tabby cat, Django.

Jeff Miner is Senior Pastor of Jesus Metropolitan Community Church, Indianapolis — one of the largest, fastest-growing Metropolitan Community Churches in the U.S. He is co-author of one of the best-selling books on homosexuality and the Bible — *The Children Are Free: Re-examining the Biblical Evidence on Same-sex Relationships* — and serves as Chair of the Board of Administration for Metropolitan Community Churches (MCC), a Christian denomination with a special outreach to LGBTQ people. Jeff has twice received MCC's Phoenix Award for Church Growth and Revitalization. Prior to becoming pastor, Jeff practiced law for thirteen years, serving as Deputy Chief Counsel for Legislative Affairs at a federal banking agency in Washington, D.C. He is an honors graduate of Harvard Law School (J.D., 1983) and Bob Jones University (B.A., 1980). He prepared for ordination in the MCC via their Samaritan Training Program over a period of years while still lawyering. Jeff lives with his partner of nineteen years, David Zier.

John Seksay moved to Indianapolis in 2001 and
started attending Jesus MCC shortly thereafter.
He became a member in 2003. His spiritual journey
has included both Christian and non-Christian
faiths prior to Jesus Metropolitan Community
Church. The landmarks in that spiritual journey
include marriage, three children, divorce, coming
out, becoming a grandparent, and finding this
spiritual home. John's career has always focused in the medical field
since starting x-ray training in 1965. He currently works as a clinical
educator for a diagnostic ultrasound manufacturer.

Julie Walsh grew up in St. Louis and was raised,
since the age of nine, as one of the few children in
MCC (before the child boom we are blessed with
today!) She moved to Indianapolis to attend Butler
University, and then began a ten-year tenure on
the staff at Jesus MCC as their Minister of Worship. She has served as an educator and consultant
for MCCs nationwide, and has also held music
teaching positions for the Department of Corrections and a local
Jesuit high school. Julie is currently on sabbatical, preparing for
the next phase of her ministry while working as an over-the-road
truck driver with her partner, Brent. When not behind the wheel,
Julie enjoys spending time working on her two books in progress for
future publication.

Kay Olry is a writer and speaker, currently residing in Indianapolis,
where she lives and loves with Dee, her spouse of seventeen years.
She hails from a large Irish Catholic family, fondly referred to as
"The Clan." A veteran of the U. S. Air Force, Kay spent five years in
the 1980s working in Radio and Television Broadcasting and Public
Affairs in posts all over the world. Her interests are wide and varied,
and include: Christianity, spirituality, LGBTQ concerns, and health

issues (especially in dealing with chronic pain management and the politics of pain). She has become an advocate through the National Fibromyalgia Association's Leaders Against Pain Coalition, and endeavors to create awareness of patient issues by educating patients, medical professionals, and the legislature. Recently Kay was required to leave her job due to health issues. She continues to write and speak, and is developing an internet community for people dealing with chronic pain and illness. The goal of the site will focus on creating hope in all areas — mental, physical, and spiritual.

Keith Phillips has been a hospice chaplain for the past eight years, having pastored American Baptist churches in Indiana for the previous twenty-five years. He was raised in New Hampshire and is a graduate of Clark University, the Earlham School of Religion, and McCormick Theological Seminary. He has a daughter, Linley, and a son, Geoffrey, both in their twenties and both of whom live in southern Indiana. His standard poodle, Black Forest, is his second-best friend. Keith joined Jesus Metropolitan Community Church in 2007 and has recently transferred his ordination credentials to the Metropolitan Community Churches.

Mark Shoup was born in Dayton, Ohio, and attended the West Charleston Church of the Brethren, as his family has done for four generations. After high school, he graduated from the Culinary Institute of America in Hyde Park, N.Y., and has worked in the food industry in both Dayton and Indianapolis, where he now resides. His career in food ended when an on-the-job back injury forced him to stop working. He now works as the Administrative Assistant in the church office of Jesus MCC. Writing has been a hobby of his since his early 20s, along with gardening, skiing, scuba, astronomy, travel, and, more recently, breeding Scottish terriers and renovating old houses. Mark is grateful for churches like Jesus Metropolitan Community Church, which strive for radical inclusive love, without which he wonders why people even bother to go to church.

Melody Merida spent much of her childhood in southern Indiana, being reared in Independent Baptist churches. She is delighted to use those experiences in her service as the Minister of Congregational Care at Jesus Metropolitan Community Church in Indianapolis, where she has been since 2007. She is currently studying for her Master of Divinity degree at Earlham School of Religion in Richmond, Indiana. Melody resides in Indianapolis with her two dogs, Annie and Baxter, and her beautiful cat, Bailey Joseph.

Morgan Stewart (not the author's real name) lives with a partner of four years in southern Indiana where they parent two pre-teen children. A former columnist, Morgan has had work published regularly for years in various newspapers, business trade journals, and spiritual venues. Morgan dreams of someday writing a book.

Pam Beutler was born during the winter of 1952 in Chicago, Illinois. She is a first-generation American, born to German-Bohemian parents. She was raised Roman Catholic, attended parochial schools, and graduated from Loyola University. She is a dog enthusiast and an avid reader.

Robert Ferguson was born and raised in Indianapolis. After attending Indiana State University
and completing a stint in the U. S. Navy, he began
a journey of spiritual enlightenment. Robert first
answered a call to ministry in a mid-sized Missionary Baptist Church. Quickly becoming disillusioned
by sexist and homophobic dogma, he soon found
his way to Jesus Metropolitan Community Church.
Currently Robert is a volunteer minister and deacon. Employed at
AT&T, Robert has returned to school in hopes of earning a degree in
religious studies.

Steve Adams joined Jesus Metropolitan Community Church in 1992. He was raised a Methodist
(mid-1950s through early 1970s), and then spent
his young adult years involved in fellowships
and classes of The Way International (mid-1970s
through late 1980s). It would take pages and pages
to name all the people who have contributed to
his spiritual journey over the years, so it's impossible to mention them here, but he is grateful for each and every one
who helped him get closer to the Lord Jesus Christ. He would like to
thank Pastor Jeff especially for his patient, diligent leadership and
for the discipleship program at Jesus MCC. Abundant thanks also go
to his supportive family and his loving spouse of sixteen years, Dan.

Theresa Benson is a Global Account Manager for a Fortune 500
semiconductor company. She is responsible for the work of people in
seventeen countries. After receiving a bachelor's degree in electrical
engineering from Iowa State University, she got a master's degree
from the school of hard knocks. She lived on the west coast for ten
years, and then her job led her to Indianapolis. She came to Jesus
Metropolitan Community Church in May 2006, following a "Would
Jesus Discriminate?" campaign. She has worked in the children's

ministry and enjoys writing for the *Be Still and Know* series. Theresa lives happily with Abby the Wonder Poodle and has recently become engaged.

Tommy Chittenden, a native Floridian and graduate of Atlanta Christian College (B.A., Cross-Cultural Communications and Youth Ministry), is the father of two adult sons who get to live with his three grandchildren in Plainfield, Indiana. A former youth minister in Atlanta, Georgia, and Plainfield, Indiana, Tommy has recently left his twenty-eight year career in the travel and entertainment arena to focus on an awakening to an entirely different outreach ministry. Working under the auspices of the National AIDS Fund in Washington, D.C., he is serving as an AmeriCorps member, assigned to Step-Up, Inc. to provide education, counseling, and testing outreach for the prevention of HIV/AIDS in the state of Indiana. He is also serving as a Discipleship teacher and Oasis (small group) leader's coach in the adult education ministry of Jesus Metropolitan Community Church.

Tyler Connoley is the child of Wesleyan missionaries, and grew up in Zambia, Africa. He has a Master of Arts in Biblical Studies from the Earlham School of Religion, where he is also pursuing a Master of Divinity so he can be ordained in the United Church of Christ. He is the coauthor with Jeff Miner of *The Children Are Free* (also from Found Pearl Press). He lives and writes in southwestern New Mexico with his spouse, Rob.

Topical Index

Scripture Index

Author Index